BRIGHT & B...
Kindergarten
Practice

Author

Suzanne Barchers, Ed.D.

SHELL EDUCATION

Publishing Credits

Dona Herweck Rice, *Editor-in-Chief*; Robin Erickson, *Production Director*;
Lee Aucoin, *Creative Director;* Timothy J. Bradley, *Illustration Manager*;
Sara Johnson, M.S.Ed, *Senior Editor*; Evelyn Garcia, *Associate Education Editor;*
Leah Quillian, *Assistant Editor;* Grace Alba, *Designer;*
Corinne Burton, *M.A.Ed., Publisher*

Standard
© 2010 National Governors Association Center for Best Practices and Council of Chief State School Officers (CCSS)

Shell Education

5301 Oceanus Drive
Huntington Beach, CA 92649-1030
http://www.shelleducation.com

ISBN 978-1-4258-0883-9

© 2012 Shell Educational Publishing, Inc.
Reprinted 2013

Table of Contents

Every Child Is Bright and Brainy

The Need for Continual Practice

"Practice makes perfect."

That's what they say, and it's usually true! Although educational practices have changed over time, some key methods have stayed the same. Children need plenty of opportunity to practice skills and show what they know. The more they do, the more they can transfer their learning to everyday life—and future success!

Of course, there has to be a good purpose for the practice. That is where the pages in this book come in. Created with the essential standards in mind, each activity page focuses on a particular concept, skill, or skill-set and provides students abundant opportunities to practice and achieve mastery.

Annis and Annis (1987) found that continual repetition helps increase the levels of the Bloom cognitive domain. In other words, practice helps students learn in a wide variety of ways at all levels of cognitive ability. It provides students opportunities to think more deeply about the subjects they are studying. Marzano (2010) asserts that in order for students to independently display their learning, it is necessary for them to practice procedural skills. Providing students with ample opportunity to practice remains a key strategy for employing the best educational practices in or out of the classroom.

Every Child Is Bright and Brainy (cont.)

Understanding the Standards

The Common Core State Standards were developed in collaboration with a wide variety of educators through the Common Core State Standards Initiative. The goal was to create a clear and consistent framework to prepare students for higher education and the workforce. To this end, teachers, school administrators, and other educational experts worked together in a state-led effort coordinated by the National Governors Association Center for Best Practices (NGA) and the Council of Chief State School Officers (CCSSO).

The standards incorporate the most effective models from around the country and around the globe, providing teachers and parents with a shared understanding of what students are expected to learn. The consistency of the standards provides a common, appropriate benchmark for students unrelated to their location.

According to the NGA and the CCSSO, these standards meet the following criteria:

- ☼ They are aligned with college and work expectations;

- ☼ They are clear, understandable, and consistent;

- ☼ They include rigorous content and application of knowledge through high-order skills;

- ☼ They build upon strengths and lessons of current state standards;

- ☼ They are informed by other top-performing countries so that all students are prepared to succeed in our global economy and society; and

- ☼ They are evidence-based

Students who meet these standards within their K–12 education should have the skills and knowledge necessary to succeed in their educational careers and beyond.

Making It Work

It is important for you to understand the key features of this book, so that you can use it in a way that works for you and your students.

- **Standards-based practice.** The exercises in *Bright & Brainy: Kindergarten Practice* are aligned with the Common Core State Standards. Each activity page focuses on a particular concept, skill, or skill-set and provides students ample opportunities to practice and achieve mastery.

- **Clear, easy-to-understand activities.** The exercises in this book are written in a kid-friendly style.

- **Assessment of student progress.** Based on student progress, the Common Core State Standards Correlation Chart (pages 9–10) helps identify the grade-level standards with which students may need additional support.

- **Reinforcement of key grade-level concepts.** Each activity provides practice of key grade-level language arts and mathematics skills in an organized and meaningful way.

- **Stand-alone activity pages.** Each activity is flexible and can be used independently in a variety of instructional or at-home settings.

The chart below provides suggestions for how to implement the activities.

Whole/Small Group	Individual	At Home/Homework
• Read and discuss the directions at the beginning of each activity. Work practice problems on an interactive whiteboard, document camera, or other display method. • Have students work problems on the interactive whiteboard. • Have students take turns reading each question. • Display the problems and review and correct them. • Read and discuss responses.	• Create folders for each student. Include a copy of their selected activity pages. • Collect work and check student answers, or provide each student with copies of the answer key and allow them to check their own work. • Select specific activity pages to support individual students' needs for additional practice.	• Provide each student with activity pages to reinforce skills. • Collect work and check student answers, or provide each student with copies of the answer key and allow them to check their own work. • Select specific activity pages to provide extra support in areas where individual students may need additional practice.

Making It Work (cont.)

Bright & Brainy: Kindergarten Practice provides practice pages for a broad range of Common Core language arts and mathematics standards. Language arts topics are designed to provide students practice in the most vital skills included in the Common Core Standards. These range from reading foundational skills to fluency, and from writing to speaking and listening. Activities designed to support student learning of how to read informational texts, literature, and vocabulary skills round out the carefully chosen exercises. Within each of these broad areas are individual activity pages centering on subtopics, such as letter recognition, alike and different, antonyms, and rhyming. Each covered skill is crucial to achieving language fluency and to setting the stage for future success in language arts. Likewise, the chosen mathematics skills represent fundamental and integral topics from the Common Core Standards. Clear, student-friendly exercises center around the essential areas of counting and cardinal numbers, number and operations in base ten, operations and algebraic thinking, measuring, data, and geometry.

Individual lessons engage students in mastering specific skills, including more, less, same, sequencing, alike and different, and flat vs. solid.

This book covers the following:

- Reading: Foundational Skills
- Language Conventions
- Reading: Informational Text
- Vocabulary Acquisition and Use
- Reading: Literature
- Fluency

- Writing
- Speaking and Listening
- Number and Operations in Base Ten
- Operations and Algebraic Thinking
- Measurement and Data
- Geometry

Additionally, the Resource CD allows for easy access to the student activity pages in this book. Electronic PDF files of all the activity pages are included on the CD.

Language Arts Activity Pages   **Mathematics Activity Pages**

Correlation to Standards

Shell Education is committed to producing educational materials that are research and standards based. In this effort, we have correlated all of our products to the academic standards of all 50 United States, the District of Columbia, the Department of Defense Dependent Schools, and all Canadian provinces. We have also correlated to the Common Core State Standards.

How to Find Standards Correlations

To print a customized correlation report of this product for your state, visit our website at **http://www.shelleducation.com** and follow the on-screen directions. If you require assistance in printing correlation reports, please contact Customer Service at 1-800-858-7339.

Purpose and Intent of Standards

Legislation mandates that all states adopt academic standards that identify the skills students will learn in kindergarten through grade twelve. Many states also have standards for Pre-K. This same legislation sets requirements to ensure the standards are detailed and comprehensive.

Standards are designed to focus instruction and guide adoption of curricula. Standards are statements that describe the criteria necessary for students to meet specific academic goals. They define the knowledge, skills, and content students should acquire at each level. Standards are also used to develop standardized tests to evaluate students' academic progress.

Teachers are required to demonstrate how their lessons meet state standards. State standards are used in development of all of our products, so educators can be assured they meet the academic requirements of each state.

Common Core State Standards

The lessons in this book are aligned to the Common Core State Standards (CCSS). The standards listed on pages 9–10 support the objectives presented throughout the lessons.

Common Core Standards Correlation Chart

Language Arts	
Reading: Foundational Skills	**Page(s)**
RF.K.1—Follow words left to right, top to bottom	11–14
RF.K.1—Understand that words are separated by spaces in print	15–18
RF.K.1—Recognize and name all upper- and lowercase letters	19, 21, 23, 25
RF.K.2—Recognize and produce rhyming words	27–30
RF.K.2—Count, pronounce, blend, and segment syllables in spoken words	31
RF.K.2—Blend and segment onsets and rimes of single-syllable spoken words	32–34
RF.K.2—Isolate and pronounce the initial, medial vowel, and final sounds	35–41
RF.K.2—Add or substitute individual sounds to make new words	42–43
RF.K.3—Associate the long and short sounds for the five major vowels	44–49
RF.K.3—Distinguish between similarly spelled words	50–57
Language Conventions	**Page(s)**
L.K.1—Print many upper- and lowercase letters	58–63
L.K.1—Use frequently occuring nouns and verbs	64–71
L.K.1—Form regular plural nouns	72–75
L.K.1—Understand and use question words	76–77
L.K.1—Use the most frequently occuring prepositions	78–79
L.K.2—Capitalize first word in sentence and the pronoun *I*	80–81
L.K.2—Recognize and name end punctuation	82–83
L.K.2—Write a letter or letters for most consonant and short-vowel sounds	84–89
Reading: Informational Text	**Page(s)**
RI.K.4—Ask and answer questions about unknown words in a text	90–93
RI.K.2—Identify the main topic and retell key details of a text	94–99
RI.K.7—Describe the relationship between illustrations and the text	100–103, 106–109
RI.K.8—Identify the reasons an author gives to support points in a text	104–105
Vocabulary Acquisition and Use	**Page(s)**
L.K.4—Use the most frequently occurring inflections and affixes as a clue	110–114
L.K.5—Sort common objects into categories to gain a sense of the concepts	115–117, 120–122
L.K.5—Demonstrate understanding of verbs and adjectives by relating them	118–119
Reading: Literature	**Page(s)**
RL.K.1—Ask and answer questions about key details in text	123–126
RL.K.3—Identify characters, settings, and major events in a story	127–128
Reading: Fluency	**Page(s)**
RF.K.4—Read emergent-reader texts with purpose and understanding	129–130
Writing	**Page(s)**
W.K.1—Use a combination of drawing and writing to compose opinion pieces	131–132
W.K.2—Use a combination of drawing and writing to compose informative text	133–134
W.K.3—Use a combination of drawing and writing to narrate a single event	135–138
Speaking and Listening	**Page(s)**
SL.K.6—Speak audibly and express thoughts, feelings, and ideas clearly	139–140

Common Core Standards Correlation Chart (cont.)

Mathematics	
Counting and Cardinality	**Page(s)**
K.CC.1—Count to 100 by ones and by tens	141–151
K.CC.5—Count to answer "how many?" questions about as many as 20 things arranged in a line, a rectangular array, or a circle, or as many as 10 things in a scattered configuration	152–174
K.CC.6—Identify whether the number of objects in one group is greater than, less than, or equal to the number of objects in another group	175–178
K.CC.7—Compare two numbers between 1 and 10 presented as written numerals	179–182
Operations and Algebraic Thinking	**Page(s)**
K.OA.1—Represent addition and subtraction with objects	183–185
K.OA.2—Solve addition and subtraction word problems, and add and subtract within 10	186–194
K.OA.3—Decompose numbers less than or equal to 10 into pairs	195–200
Number and Operations in Base Ten	**Page(s)**
K.NBT.1—Compose and decompose numbers from 11 to 19	201–202
Measurement and Data	**Page(s)**
K.MD.1—Describe measurable attributes of objects	203, 205
K.MD.2—Directly compare two objects with a measureable attribute	204, 206
K.MD.3—Classify objects into given categories	207–210
Geometry	**Page(s)**
K.G.1—Describe objects in the environment using names of shapes	211–214
K.G.2—Correctly name shapes regardless of their orientations	215–218
K.G.3—Identify shapes as two-dimensional or three-dimensional	219–224
K.G.4—Analyze and compare two- and three-dimensional shapes	225–226
K.G.6—Compose simple shapes	227

Name: _____ **Date:** _____

Draw the Line

....

Directions: Draw a line through all the pictures that are alike.

1

airplane   airplane   apple   airplane

2

can   can   can   car

3

bee   ball   ball   ball

4

dad   dad   dad   dad

Name: _____ **Date:** _____

Follow These!

Directions: Draw a line through all the pictures that are alike.

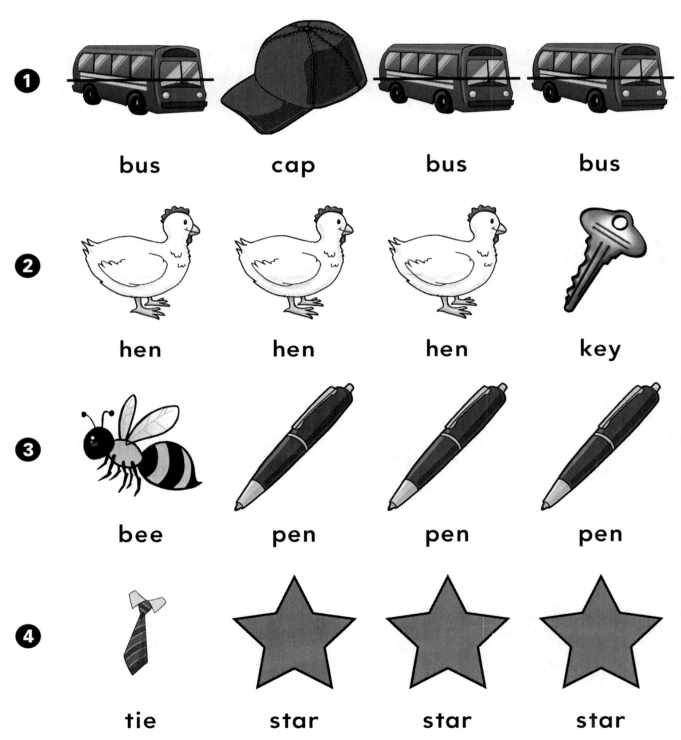

1   bus   cap   bus   bus

2   hen   hen   hen   key

3   bee   pen   pen   pen

4   tie   star   star   star

Name: _____ Date: _____

Is It the Same?

Directions: Draw a line through all the pictures that are alike.

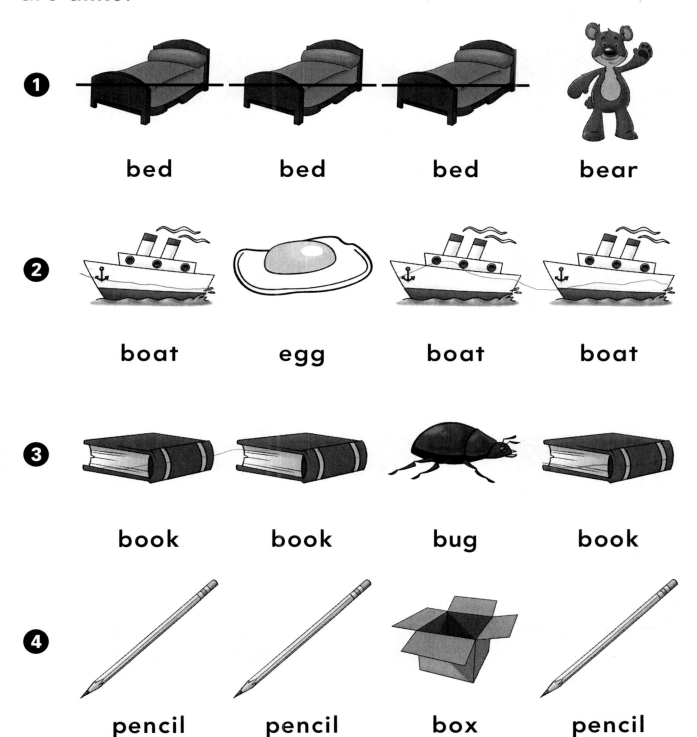

1

bed   bed   bed   bear

2

boat   egg   boat   boat

3

book   book   bug   book

4

pencil   pencil   box   pencil

Name: _____ **Date:** _____

Find the Same Pictures

. . . .

Directions: Draw a line through all the pictures that are alike.

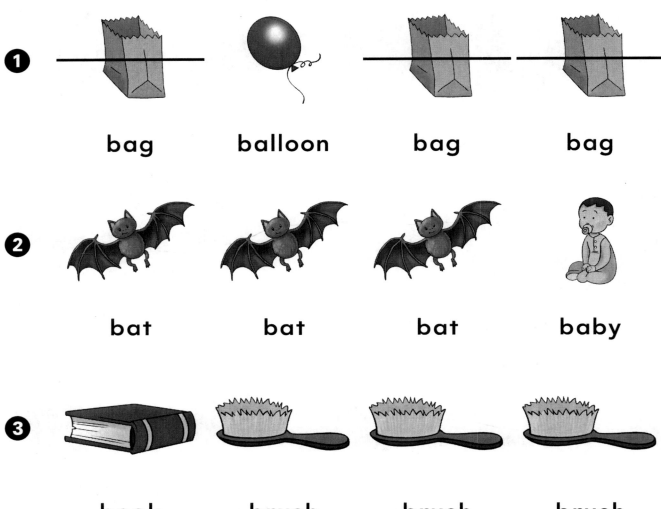

①

bag   balloon   bag   bag

②

bat   bat   bat   baby

③

book   brush   brush   brush

④

cat   cat   cat   cat

Name: _____ **Date:** _____

Missing Words!

Directions: Choose a word to finish the sentence.

~~can~~   bee   car   dad

1 This is a _____ can _____ .

2 This is a _____ .

3 This is a _____ .

4 This is a _____ .

Name: _____ **Date:** _____

Which Word?

Directions: Choose a word to finish the sentence.

~~bed~~   hat   box   cat

1   This is a ___ bed ___ .

2   This is a _____ .

3   This is a _____ .

4   This is a _____ .

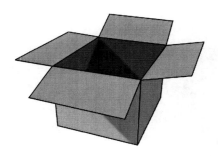

Name: _____ Date: _____

Write It Right

Directions: Choose a sentence that matches the picture.

~~This is a baby.~~

This is a duck.

This is a shoe.

1 This is a baby.

2

3

Name: _____ **Date:** _____

Write More

. . . .

Directions: Choose a sentence that matches the picture.

~~This is a bear.~~

This is a shoe.

This is a book.

1   This is a bear.

2   _____

3   _____

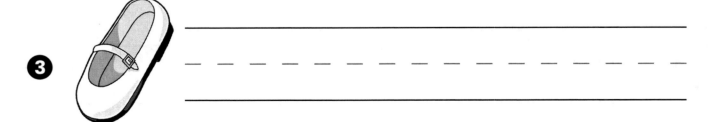

Lowercase Letter Match

Directions: Cut out the letters. Turn them over. Play a matching game.

a	a	b	b
c	c	d	d
e	e	f	f
g	g	h	h
i	i	j	j
k	k	l	l
m	m	n	n

This page is intended to be left blank.

Name: _____ **Date:** _____

More Lowercase Letter Match

Directions: Cut out the letters. Turn them over. Play a matching game.

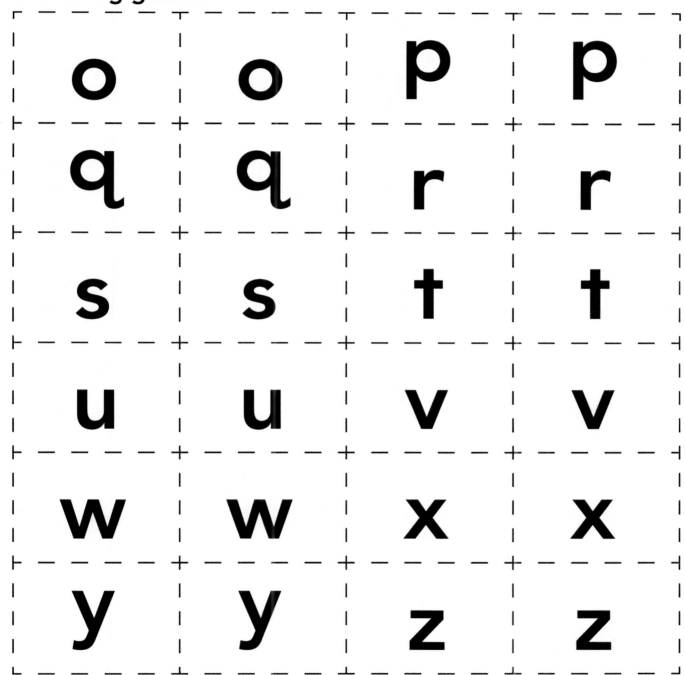

This page is intended to be left blank.

Capital Letter Match

Directions: Cut out the letters. Turn them over. Play a matching game.

A	A	B	B
C	C	D	D
E	E	F	F
G	G	H	H
I	I	J	J
K	K	L	L
M	M	N	N

This page is intended to be left blank.

More Capital Letter Match

Directions: Cut out the letters. Turn them over. Play a matching game.

O	O	P	P
Q	Q	R	R
S	S	T	T
U	U	V	V
W	W	X	X
Y	Y	Z	Z

This page is intended to be left blank.

Name: _____ **Date:** _____

Rhyme Time

Directions: Say the name of the picture in the box. Circle the picture that rhymes.

1   (pan)

2

3

4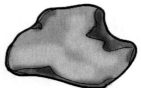

Name: _____ **Date:** _____

More Rhyme Time

Directions: Say the name of the picture in the box. Circle the picture that rhymes.

1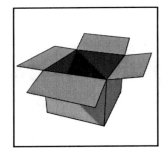

2

3

4

Name: _____ **Date:** _____

Find the Rhyme

. . . .

Directions: Say the name of the picture in the box. Circle the picture that rhymes.

1

2

3

4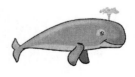

Name: _____ **Date:** _____

Find These Rhymes

Directions: Say the name of the picture in the box. Circle the picture that rhymes.

1

2

3

4

Name: _____ **Date:** _____

How Many Parts?

. . . .

Directions: Write 1 if the word has one part. Write 2 if the word has two parts.

❶

❷

❸

❹

❺

❻

Name: _____ **Date:** _____

What Is That Sound?

....

Directions: Circle the pictures that start with the letter.

b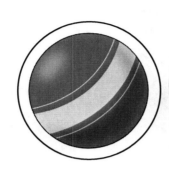

c

d

f

Name: _____ **Date:** _____

Name That Letter Sound

Directions: Circle the pictures that start with the letter.

k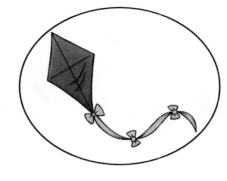

l

m

n

Name: _____ **Date:** _____

Name More Letter Sounds

Directions: Circle the pictures that start with the letter.

S

t

v

w

Name: _____ Date: _____

Beginning Sounds

Directions: Circle the correct letter to start the word.

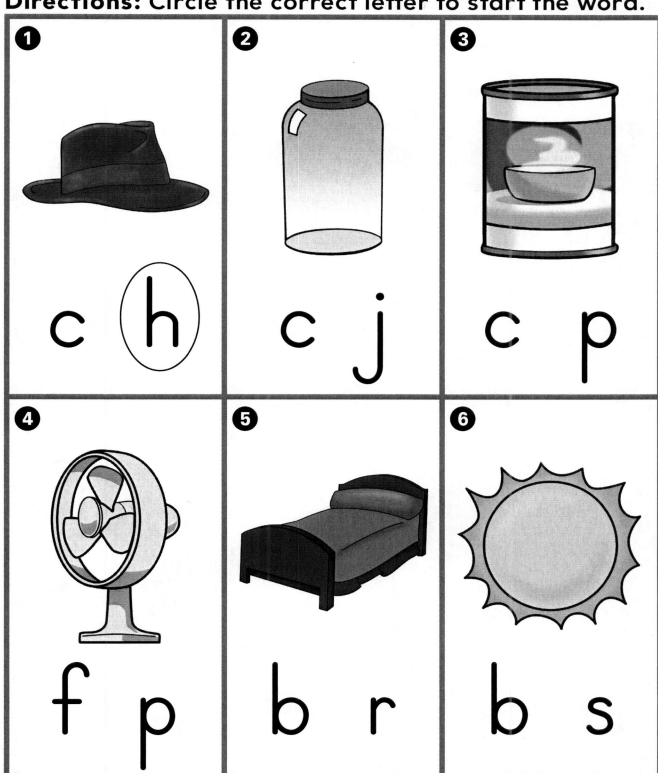

① c (h)

② c j

③ c p

④ f p

⑤ b r

⑥ b s

Name: _____ **Date:** _____

More Beginning Sounds

Directions: Circle the correct letter to start the word.

1

(d) l

2

b f

3

h p

4

h t

5

p w

6

b c

Name: _____ Date: _____

Even More Beginning Sounds

Directions: Circle the correct letter to start the word.

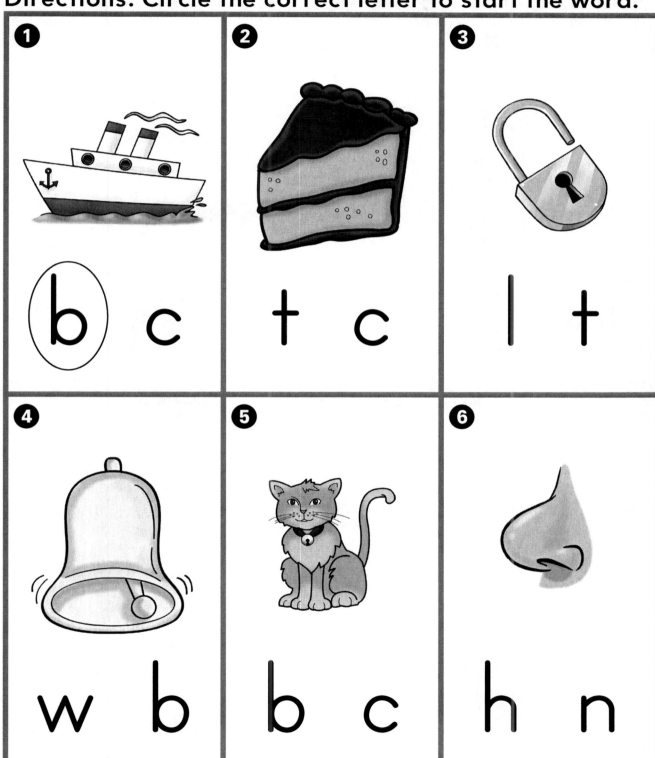

Name: _____ **Date:** _____

Make New Words!

Directions: Cross out the first letter. Circle the picture that matches the new word.

1

block

2

farm

3

stop

4

train

Name: _____ **Date:** _____

What Sound?

Directions: Choose a letter to complete each word.

~~b~~   c   p   s

1

b̲ed

2

_____an

3

_____un

4

_____at

Name: _____ **Date:** _____

Missing Letter

Directions: Choose a letter to complete each word.

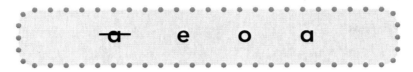

~~a~~   e   o   a

❶

c __a__ n

❷

b ___ x

❸

b ___ g

❹

b ___ e

Name: _____ **Date:** _____

Word Endings

Directions: Choose a letter to complete each word.

> d g n +

1

ha **+**

2

pe _____

3

pi _____

4

be _____

Name: _____ Date: _____

New Words

Directions: A new word is made by changing one letter. Write the new word.

1

mom

mop

2

hat

_____

3

cap

_____

4

map

_____

Name: _____ **Date:** _____

More New Words

Directions: A new word is made by changing one letter. Write the new word.

1 hen _____

pen

2 wig _____

3 coat _____

4 jar _____

Name: _____ **Date:** _____

Name That Short Vowel

. . . .

Directions: Circle all the pictures that have the short *a* sound.

Name: _____ Date: _____

Name More Short Vowels

Directions: Circle all the pictures that have the short *i* sound.

Name: _____ **Date:** _____

Can You Name That Short Vowel?

Directions: Circle all the pictures that have the short *u* sound.

Name: _____ **Date:** _____

Name That Long Vowel

Directions: Circle all the pictures that have the long *a* sound.

Name: _____ **Date:** _____

Name More Long Vowels

Directions: Circle all the pictures that have the long *i* sound.

Name: _____ Date: _____

Can You Name These Long Vowels?

Directions: Circle all the pictures that have the long *u* sound.

Name: _____ **Date:** _____

Read Tricky Words

Directions: Choose the right word to finish the sentence.

are	~~have~~	I	like

1 I __have__ a hen.

2 _____ am a boy.

3 I _____ my cat.

4 They _____ kids.

Name: _____ Date: _____

Find the Right Word

Directions: Choose the right word to finish the sentence.

~~Do~~   with   is   have

1 D o _____ you like apples?

2 I _____ a ball.

3 The bed _____ big.

4 He is _____ the girl.

Name: _____ **Date:** _____

Read Even More Tricky Words

Directions: Choose the right word to finish the sentence.

| Do | He | ~~The~~ | They |

1 ___The___ pig is fat.

2 _____ you like frogs?

3 _____ are red.

4 _____ likes to run.

#50883—Bright & Brainy: Kindergarten Practice

Name: _____ Date: _____

Use Tricky Words

Directions: Choose the right word to finish the sentence.

| for | not | that | ~~was~~ |

1 The ball ___was___ in the box.

2 The bow is _____ me.

3 An ant is _____ big.

4 What is in _____ tub?

Name: _____ **Date:** _____

Spell Tricky Words

Directions: Pick the right word to finish the sentence.

❶ I _____ saw _____ a pet.

saw   said

❷ It was a _____.

can   cat

❸ The cat was _____.

big   dig

❹ The cat _____ fur.

had   hat

Name: _____ Date: _____

Spell More Tricky Words

Directions: Pick the right word to finish the sentence.

1 I _____have_____ a pet.

have   has

2 It _____ a dog.

if   is

3 _____ name is Lucky.

Her   Here

4 I _____ a cat, too.

what   want

Name: _____ **Date:** _____

Choose the Tricky Word

Directions: Pick the right word to finish the sentence.

❶ I  _____ to the farm.

    what   went

❷ I _____ a pig.

    was   saw

❸ He _____ in a pen.

    was   saw

❹ I _____ pigs.

    lick   like

Name: _____ **Date:** _____

Choose More Tricky Words

Directions: Pick the right word to finish the sentence.

1 __Look_____ at that man!

　　　Like　　　Look

2 His job is _____.

　　　　　　fun　　　fur

3 His nose _____ big.

　　　　looks　　　likes

4 He has a hat, _____.

　　　　　　two　　　too

Name: _____ **Date:** _____

Practice Your Letters

....

Directions: Trace the letters.

R r   G g   J j

M m   N n   T t

Name: _____ **Date:** _____

Practice More Letters

Directions: Trace the letters.

A a   D d   B b

O o   Q q   P p

Name: _____ **Date:** _____

Practice Even More Letters

Directions: Trace the letters.

Name: _____ **Date:** _____

Lots of Letters

··

Directions: Trace the letters.

Name: _____ **Date:** _____

Trace More Letters

Directions: Trace the letters.

Name: _____ Date: _____

Keep Tracing

Directions: Trace the letters.

Yy   Hh   Ff

Hh   Rr   Ee

Name: _____ **Date:** _____

Which Word Is Right?

....

Directions: Choose the right word to finish the sentence.

1	That is a big __bat__ . hat bat
2	The _____ is full. car can
3	_____ has a bag. Dad Mom
4	_____ is tall. Dad Mom

Name: _____ Date: _____

Choose the Right Word

Directions: Choose the right word to finish the sentence.

1 That is a big ___dog___ .

hat   dog

2 The _____ has a toy.

baby   mom

3 The _____ is blue.

fish   bird

4 I ride the _____ .

bus   car

Name: _____ **Date:** _____

Which Word?

....

Directions: Choose the right word to finish the sentence.

① 	The ___hen___ is white. hen dog
② 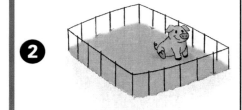	The pig is in the _____. pen car
③ 	The _____ is brown. fish house
④ 	The man has a _____. dog book

Name: _____ Date: _____

Choose More Words

Directions: Choose the right word to finish the sentence.

1	The ____ant____ is black. ant green
2	The eggs are on a _____ . dish cup
3	Birds live in a _____ . net nest
4	The dog is in a _____ . tub bed

Name: _____ **Date:** _____

Finish the Sentence

Directions: Choose the right word to finish the sentence.

1 	The duck  .	flaps begs
2	The dog _____ .	hops wags
3	The fish _____ .	digs swims
4	The frog _____ .	hops hugs

Name: _____ Date: _____

What Do These Pictures Say?

Directions: Choose the right word to finish the sentence.

1 The girl rides her bike.

rides runs

2 The boy _____ .

runs falls

3 The boy _____ .

digs naps

4 The girl _____ .

claps reads

Name: _____ Date: _____

Read Carefully!

. . . .

Directions: Choose the right word to finish the sentence.

1

The boat ___moves___.

moves sinks

2

The girl _____.

skips stops

3

The bus _____.

claps stops

4

The plane _____.

falls flies

Name: _____ **Date:** _____

Read These Carefully!

Directions: Choose the right word to finish the sentence.

1	The baby _plays_ . naps plays
2	The mom _____ . hugs sings
3	The boy _____ . falls draws
4	The girl _____ . rests grows

Name: _____ **Date:** _____

One or Two?

The first picture says *hen*. The second picture says *hens* because there is more than one.

hen

hens

Directions: Circle the right word for each picture.

1 pig   pigs

2 hat   hats

3 pan   pans

4 sun   suns

Name: _____ **Date:** _____

More Than One?

The first picture says *boy*. The second picture says *boys* because there is more than one.

boy   boys

Directions: Circle the right word for each picture.

1

bed   beds

2

apple   apples

3

can   cans

4

nut   nuts

Name: _____ **Date:** _____

How Many in These?

> The first picture says *box*. The second picture says *boxes* because there is more than one.

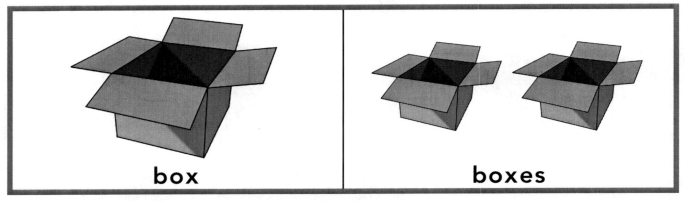

box   boxes

Directions: Circle the right word for each picture.

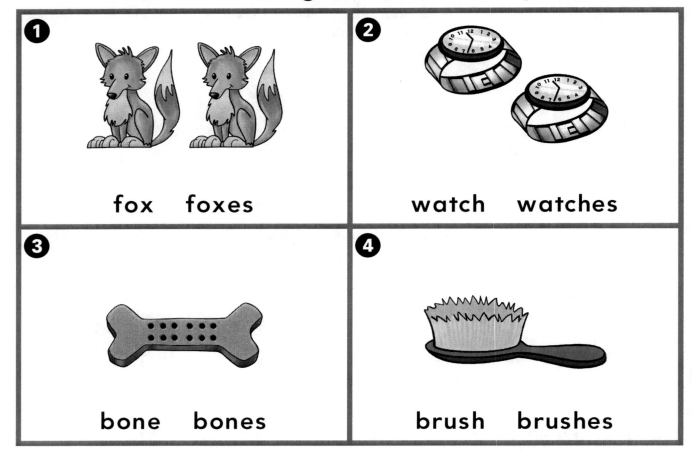

❶ fox   foxes

❷ watch   watches

❸ bone   bones

❹ brush   brushes

Name: _____ Date: _____

More Plural Practice

The first picture says *ring*. The second picture says *rings* because there is more than one.

| ring | rings |

Directions: Circle the right word for each picture.

1 tree   trees

2 sock   socks

3 lock   locks

4 coat   coats

Name: _____ **Date:** _____

Finish the Questions

Directions: Write the missing word for each question.

Who   What

1 ___W h a t_____ is on the card?

_____

2 _____ is the boy?

_____

3 _____ does the boy have?

_____

4 _____ has the cards?

Name: _____ Date: _____

Finish More Questions

Directions: Write the missing word for each question.

| Where | Who |

1 W̲h̲e̲r̲e̲ will they go?

2 _____ is stopped?

3 _____ is going?

4 _____ is the cone?

Name: _____ **Date:** _____

Where Is It?

Directions: Write the missing word for each question.

on	by

_____

❶ The food is _____ on _____ the tray.

❷ The peas are _____ the milk.

❸ The cake is _____ the dish.

❹ The meat is _____ the peas.

Name: _____ Date: _____

Where Are They?

Directions: Write the missing word for each question.

in   by

_____

1 They are _____ in _____ the car.

2 The girl is _____ the boy.

3 The boy is _____ the window.

4 They are _____ their seats.

Name: _____ **Date:** _____

Capital Mistake

Directions: Put a check by the sentence with the capital letter mistake.

1 I have a dog. ☐

i have a dog. ✓

2 My dog has spots. ☐

my dog has spots. ☐

3 May i pet your dog? ☐

May I pet your dog? ☐

4 your dog is big! ☐

Your dog is big! ☐

Name: _____ **Date:** _____

Capitalize It

Directions: Circle the words that need a capital letter.

(i)like my cats. they are fun. i give my cats toys. They like toys. max is white. he likes to play with yarn. Sox likes mice. she and Max are fun.

Name: _____ Date: _____

Punctuate the Sentences

Sentences end with a period, question mark, or exclamation point. This is what each looks like:

.

?

!

period   question mark   exclamation point

Directions: Circle the punctuation mark at the end of each sentence.

1 Do you like apples?

.   (?)   !

2 I love apples!

.   ?   !

3 I have ten apples.

.   ?   !

4 Can you count to ten?

.   ?   !

Name: _____ Date: _____

Punctuate More Sentences

A sentence ends with a period, question mark, or exclamation point. This is what each looks like:

.	?	!
period	question mark	exclamation point

Directions: Write a period, question mark, or exclamation point at the end of each sentence.

Do you know how to snap _?_____

I do _____

It can be hard _____

I like to snap _____

Name: _____ **Date:** _____

Name the Short Vowels

· ·

Directions: Write the missing letter in the blank.

❶

c ◯ n

❷

m ___ p

❸

b ___ g

❹

b ___ g

Name: _____ **Date:** _____

Name More Short Vowels

Directions: Write the missing letter in the blank.

❶

b _o_ ll

❷

l ___ d

❸

d ___ ck

❹

b ___ x

Name: _____ **Date:** _____

Spelling Fun

Directions: Write the missing letter in the blank.

1

c ___ r

2

s ___ n

3

l ___ g

4

c ___ p

Name: _____ **Date:** _____

More Spelling Words

Directions: Spell each picture.

Name: _____ **Date:** _____

Keep Spelling!

Directions: Spell each picture.

1

_____ _____ _____

c a p

2

_____ _____ _____

3

_____ _____ _____

4

_____ _____ _____

Name: _____ **Date:** _____

Keep Spelling More Words!

Directions: Spell each picture.

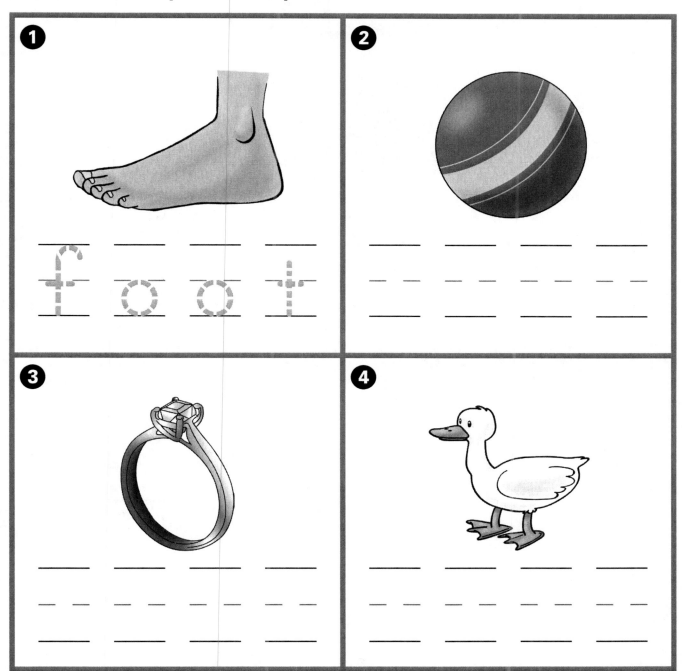

①

f o o t

②

③

④

Name: _____ **Date:** _____

Ben the Elephant

Directions: Read the story. Then, answer the questions.

Ben is a big elephant. Ben eats grass. He picks it up with his trunk. Ben smells with his trunk, too.

_____

_ _ _ _ _ _ _ _ _ _ _ _

❶ What is the elephant's name? _____

_____

_ _ _ _ _ _ _ _ _ _ _ _

❷ What does he eat? _____

_____

_ _ _ _ _ _ _ _ _ _ _ _

❸ What does he use to pick up food? _____

_____

_ _ _ _ _ _ _ _ _ _ _ _

❹ What does he use to smell? _____

Name: _____ Date: _____

Pal the Dog

Directions: Read the story. Then, answer the questions.

Pal is a dog. Pal can open the door. He can get Pete's shoes. He helps Pete a lot. He is a really good friend!

_____

- - - - - - - - - - - - - - - - -

❶ What kind of animal is Pal? _____

_____

- - - - - - - - - - - - - - - - -

❷ What does Pal open? _____

_____

- - - - - - - - - - - - - - - - -

❸ What does Pal get? _____

_____

- - - - - - - - - - - - - - - - -

❹ Why is Pal a good friend? _____

_____

- - - - - - - - - - - - - - - - -

_____

Name: _____ **Date:** _____

Ducks!

Directions: Read the story. Then, answer the questions.

A mother duck is called a hen. She uses her own feathers in the nest. She may lay ten eggs. The babies hatch in 4 weeks. The babies are called ducklings.

❶ What is a mother duck called? _____

❷ What does the mother use feathers for? _____

❸ How many weeks does it take for babies to hatch? _____

❹ What are babies called? _____

Name: _____ Date: _____

Frogs Are Neat

Directions: Read the story. Then, answer the questions.

A baby frog is a tadpole. It starts as an egg. It has to stay in water. A tadpole uses its tail to move. It has very tiny teeth. It finds food in the water. The tadpole takes more than 12 weeks to grow up.

1 What is a baby frog? _____

2 Where does it live? _____

3 How does it move? _____

4 Where does it find food? _____

Name: _____ **Date:** _____

The Big Idea

Directions: Read the story. Circle the best title.

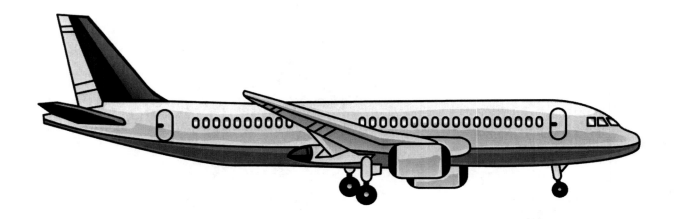

The jet is fast. It flies high in the sky. It can hold lots of people. It can fly a long ways.

The best title is:

    a.   All About Jets

    b.   Jets and Trains

    c.   People on Jets

Name: _____ Date: _____

What's the Big Idea?

Directions: Read the story. Circle the best title.

Snakes can be long or short. Snakes eat mice. Their skin is soft and dry. Some snakes are safe. They can be good pets.

The best title is:

a. What Do Snakes Eat?

b. What Are Snakes Like?

c. Why Snakes Are Bad

Name: _____ **Date:** _____

Another Big Idea

Directions: Read the story. Circle the best title.

Many babies drink milk. Cows and goats feed milk to their babies. So do dogs and cats. Even monkeys drink milk!

The best title is:

a. Milk Comes in Bottles

b. At the Farm

c. Milk Is for Babies

Name: _____ Date: _____

Help the Author

Directions: Read the story. Circle the best title.

Some boats are for fun. Some are for work. This boat tugs big boats. Some boats are broken down. That is when the tugboat goes to work.

The best title is:

a. A Working Boat

b. A Broken Boat

c. Boat Fun

Name: _____ **Date:** _____

Give the Story a Title

Directions: Read the story. Circle the best title.

Birds work hard for their babies. The mom lays the eggs. She keeps the eggs warm. She feeds the babies after they hatch. Then, she teaches them to fly.

The best title is:

a. How Birds Fly

b. How to Raise a Baby Bird

c. Big Bird Nests

Name: _____ Date: _____

Give This Story a Title

Directions: Read the story. Circle the best title.

Pigs are smart animals. You can train a pig. It can learn to sit. It can learn to stay. A pig learns fast with treats.

The best title is:

a. Feeding Pigs

b. Pigs on the Farm

c. Smart Pigs!

Name: _____ **Date:** _____

Tell About the Picture

Directions: Circle the sentence that matches the picture.

The cat has a fish.

The cat has yarn.

The dog has a bone.

The dog begs.

The kids look at the bell.

The kids ring the bell.

Name: _____ **Date:** _____

What Does the Picture Tell?

Directions: Circle the sentence that matches the picture.

The girls smile.

The girls cry.

Dad has a bag.

Dad has a pan.

The boy takes a nap.

The boy takes a drink.

Name: _____ **Date:** _____

What Does the Picture Show?

Directions: Circle the sentence that matches the picture.

Jan pats her desk.

Jan sings at her desk.

Bob is on a stage.

Bob is at the mall.

Niko walks home.

Niko runs home.

Name: _____ **Date:** _____

Tell About These Pictures

Directions: Circle the sentence that matches the picture.

1

José dances! He is sad.

José swims! He is happy.

2

Jim tip toes.

Jim reads.

3

Sara rides her bike.

Sara runs.

Name: _____ **Date:** _____

Tom's Story

Directions: Read what Tom wrote. Then, answer the question.

Some kids do not like bats. I do. Can you fly fast? Bats can. Can you sleep upside down? Bats can. Can you catch bugs in the air? Bats can. I like bats.

Why does Tom like bats?

_____

- -

_____

- -

_____

#50883—Bright & Brainy: Kindergarten Practice

© Shell Education

Name: _____ Date: _____

Pat's Story

Directions: Read what Pat wrote. Then, answer the question.

Can you run up the wall? A mouse can. Its tail helps it climb. Its tail is as long as its body. Mice can do tricks. They like to nap in a box. Mice are fun!

Why does Pat think mice are fun?

_____

_____

_____

_____

_____

Name: _____ **Date:** _____

Be a Sentence Detective

Directions: Circle the picture that goes with the sentence.

❶ The duck quacks.

❷ The brush is on the table.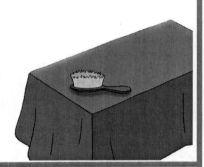

❸ She uses the fan.

❹ The fish is in the pan.

Name: _____ Date: _____

Detect More Meanings

Directions: Circle the picture that goes with the sentence.

❶ The key goes in the lock.

❷ Dad paints the bird house.

❸ My new pet is a dog.

❹ Dad rakes the grass.

Name: _____ Date: _____

Detect Even More Meanings

Directions: Circle the picture that goes with the sentence.

1 The pig is in the pen.

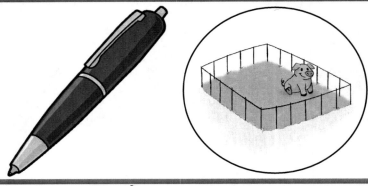

2 He rings the bell.

3 He saws the log.

4 She can skate on the ice.

Name: _____ Date: _____

Figure It Out

Directions: Circle the picture that goes with the sentence.

1 He will sled down the hill.

2 Tie your shoes.

3 The child plays with the top.

4 The bowl is clean.

Name: _____   **Date:** _____

Prefix Practice

··

A **prefix** is a word part added to the beginning of a word. It changes the meaning. The prefix *un-* means not.

Directions: Add the prefix *un-* to each word. Then, choose the sentence that matches.

1 ___un___ pin	✓ a. I take a pin off my dress. ___ b. I pin up my dress.
2 _____ fair	___ a. The boy takes a toy from a baby. ___ b. The boy gives a toy to a baby.
3 _____ box	___ a. Dad takes the pan out of the box. ___ b. Dad puts the pan in the box.
4 _____ tie	___ a. I take the bow off the box. ___ b. I put a bow on the box.

Name: _____ Date: _____

More Prefix Practice

A **prefix** is a word part added to the beginning of a word. It changes the meaning. The prefix *re-* means again.

Directions: Add the prefix *re-* to each word. Then, choose the sentence that matches.

_____heat   _____fill

__re__do   _____glue

1 Mom, will you _____redo_____ my hair?

2 Sam, my plane broke again. _____

Will you _____ it?

3 The boy wants a drink. _____

Will you _____ his glass?

4 The soup is cold. _____

Please _____ it.

Name: _____ **Date:** _____

Practice with *Pre-*

A **prefix** is a word part added to the beginning of a word. It changes the meaning. The prefix *pre-* means before.

Directions: Choose the word that matches the sentence.

prechill	preheat
precut	prewash

❶ The food must stay cold.

 the dish.

_____

_ _ _ _ _ _ _ _ _ _

❷ That top has mud on it. _____ it.

_____

_ _ _ _ _ _ _ _ _ _

❸ The oven must be hot. _____ it.

❹ The bits of apple must be small.

_____

_ _ _ _ _ _ _ _ _ _

Please _____ them.

Name: _____ **Date:** _____

Suffix Practice

A **suffix** is a word part added to the end of a word. It changes the meaning. The suffix *-ful* means full of.

Directions: Choose the word that matches the sentence.

careful	playful
helpful	~~skillful~~

1 He plays the flute well.

_____

He is __skillful__.

2 Do not fall down. Be _____.

3 The dog jumps up. It is _____.

4 Jack gave the baby his toy.

_____

Jack is _____.

Name: _____ **Date:** _____

Show the Past

Add -*ed* to a word to show the past.

Directions: Choose the word that matches the sentence.

pulled	stayed
mixed	~~worked~~

1 I ___worked___ hard to get done.

2 I _____ up the eggs.

3 He _____ on his shoes.

4 Mom got sick. She _____ home.

Name: _____ **Date:** _____

Sort the Words

Directions: Draw lines from the people to the house. Draw lines from the animals to the barn.

house

pig   **duck**   **man**   **goat**   **baby**   **woman**

barn

Name: _____ **Date:** _____

Sort More Words

Directions: Draw lines from the things that move to the wheel. Draw lines from the food to the plate.

wheel

peas   bus   milk   nut   apple   car

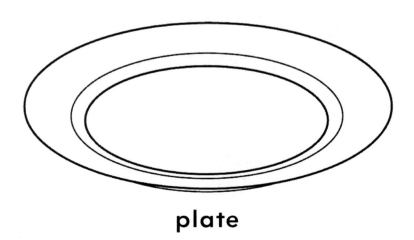

plate

Name: _____ **Date:** _____

Keep Sorting!

Directions: Draw lines from the color words to the crayon. Draw lines from the shape words to the box.

crayon

square   red   circle   triangle   orange   black

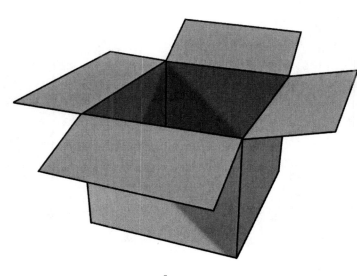

box

Name: _____ **Date:** _____

Opposites

....

Antonyms are words that mean the opposite.

Directions: Choose the word that matches each picture.

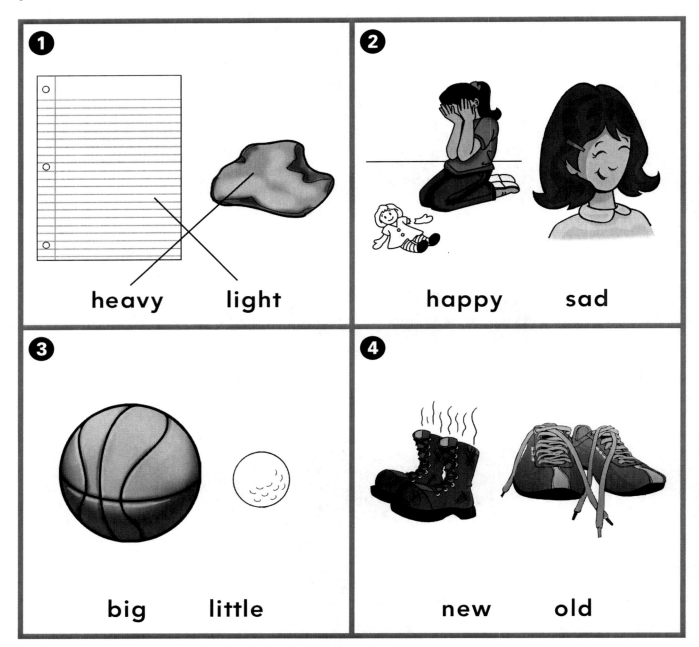

1. heavy   light

2. happy   sad

3. big   little

4. new   old

Name: _____ Date: _____

More Opposites

Antonyms are words that mean the opposite.

Directions: Choose the word that matches each picture.

1

down   up

2

fat   thin

3

asleep   awake

4

cold   hot

Name: _____ **Date:** _____

Inside or Outside?

Directions: Draw lines from the words to the best picture.

outside

bed   **tree**   **grass**   **lamp**   **sun**   **dresser**

inside

Name: _____ Date: _____

Farm or School?

Directions: Draw lines from the words to the best picture.

school

hen   book   cow   desk   horse   crayon

barn

Name: _____ **Date:** _____

Your Body

. . . .

Directions: Draw lines to where it is on the body.

leg   hand

ear   foot

arm   head

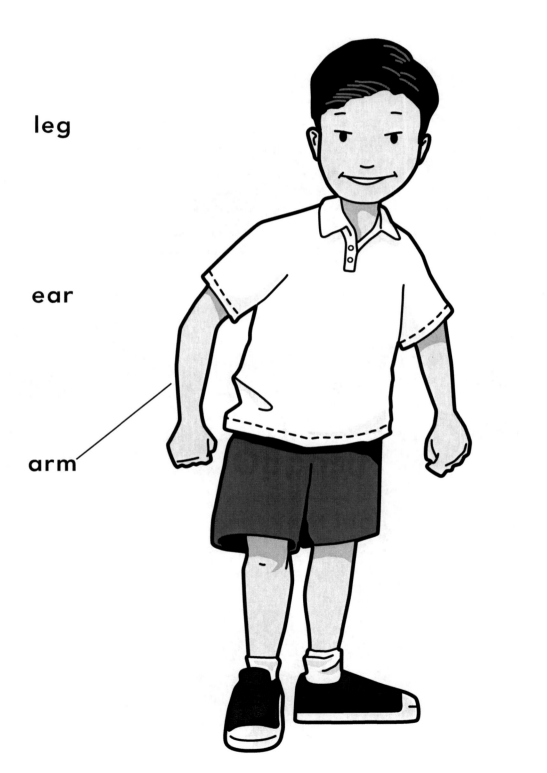

Name: _____ Date: _____

What's the Answer?

Directions: Read the story. Then, answer the questions.

> Mom gives Jack a box. It has a toy in it. Mom tells Jack three things about the toy. It is little. It has a big sail. Jack can use it in the tub. Jack likes his toy!

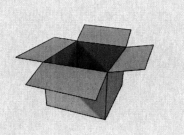

1 What is the toy in?
- a. a box
- b. a tub
- c. a car

3 Where can Jack sail his toy?
- a. in the tub
- b. in the bed
- c. in the yard

2 What size is the toy?
- a. big
- b. little
- c. huge

4 What is the toy?
- a. train
- b. jump rope
- c. sailboat

Name: _____ **Date:** _____

Find the Answers

....

Directions: Read the story. Then, answer the questions.

> Pat likes to go to the park. He runs on the grass. He digs in the sand. He runs after a duck. He jumps up on a bench. Pat has fun!

❶ Where does Pat go?
a. for a walk
b. to the sandbox
c. to the park

❸ What does Pat run after?
a. a duck
b. a friend
c. a cat

❷ What does Pat do on the grass?
a. dig
b. jump
c. run

❹ What does Pat jump up on?
a. a bench
b. the grass
c. the sand

Name: _____ Date: _____

Questions to Answer

Directions: Read the story. Then, answer the questions.

Jan likes to help Mom. She puts soap in the tub. She adds toys. She adds water. Jan gets in. Mom says, "Jan! This does not help! Get the mop!"

1 What does Jan like to do?
- **a.** take a bath
- **b.** help Mom
- **c.** mop up

2 What did Jan put in the tub first?
- **a.** toys
- **b.** water
- **c.** soap

3 What happens when Jan gets in the tub?
- **a.** Mom gets soap.
- **b.** The water spills.
- **c.** Mom mops.

4 How do you think Mom feels?
- **a.** happy
- **b.** mad
- **c.** funny

Name: _____ **Date:** _____

Read the Answer

Directions: Read the story. Then, answer the questions.

Tim has a new pet. He did not get it at a pet shop. The pet came to Tim's house. The pet made a brown home near Tim's window. The pet is blue. Guess what it is!

❶ Tim did not get his pet at a pet shop. Why not?
   a. His mom gave it to him.
   b. It came to Tim's house.
   c. It came in the window.

❷ Where did it make its home?
   a. in Tim's room
   b. in Tim's box
   c. near Tim's window

❸ What color is the pet?
   a. gray
   b. blue
   c. brown

❹ The pet's home is in a tree. What kind of home is it?
   a. a nest
   b. a den
   c. a hole

Name: _____ **Date:** _____

Book Log

Directions: Read a book. Then, fill out the form below.

Title of book: _____

_____

People in the book: _____

_____

Places in the book: _____

_____

Name: _____ **Date:** _____

Opposite Characters

....

Directions: Read a fairy tale. Choose two characters. Use words from the list to show how they are different.

| big or little | fast or slow | sad or happy |
| boy or girl | good or bad | |

Character One	Character Two
_____	_____
_ _ _ _ _ _ _	_ _ _ _ _ _ _
_____	_____
_____	_____
_ _ _ _ _ _ _	_ _ _ _ _ _ _
_____	_____
_____	_____
_ _ _ _ _ _ _	_ _ _ _ _ _ _
_____	_____
_____	_____
_ _ _ _ _ _ _	_ _ _ _ _ _ _
_____	_____
_____	_____
_ _ _ _ _ _ _	_ _ _ _ _ _ _
_____	_____
_____	_____
_ _ _ _ _ _ _	_ _ _ _ _ _ _
_____	_____

Name: _____ **Date:** _____

Be a Great Reader!

Directions: Try these ideas to be a good reader.

- Do not skip words you do not know. Ask for help and get them right next time.

- Read in the characters' voices.

- Read in a loud or soft voice.

- Read like you are on the radio.

- Read and record the book. Play it for someone in your family.

- Read the book like a chant.

- Read in a silly voice.

- Read like it is a great movie.

Name: _____ **Date:** _____

More Tips for Being a Great Reader

Directions: Find a partner. Try these ideas to be a good reader.

- Read one page aloud. Have your partner read the next page.

- Read in the characters' voices.

- Read the book aloud together.

- One reads the book. The other acts it out.

- Turn the book into a play. Add music.

- Have a good reader read part of the book. Then, read it the same way.

- Take turns making up new endings.

- Be television reporters and read the book aloud.

Name: _____ **Date:** _____

My Good Book!

· ·

Directions: Write about why you like a book.

_____

Title of book: _____

_____

This is why I like the book: _____

_____

_____

_____

_____

_____

_____

_____

_____

_____

Name: _____ **Date:** _____

My Book Review

....

Directions: Write about why you did not like a book.

_____

– – – – – – – – – – – – – – – – – – – –

Title of book: _____

_____

– – – – – – – – – – – – – – – – – – – –

This is why I did not like the book: _____

_____

– –

_____

_____

– –

_____

_____

– –

_____

_____

– –

_____

_____

– –

_____

_____

– –

_____

Name: _____ **Date:** _____

About a Pet

Directions: Write sentences to tell about a pet.

Kind of Pet

_____

- -

_____

_____

- -

_____

Name of Pet

_____

- -

_____

_____

- -

_____

What It Eats

_____

- -

_____

_____

- -

_____

Best Thing About It

_____

- -

_____

_____

- -

_____

Name: _____ **Date:** _____

My Review

Directions: Write sentences to tell about a book or movie.

Name of Book or Movie

_____

- - - - - - - - - - - - - - - - - -

_____

_____

- - - - - - - - - - - - - - - - - -

_____

Setting

_____

- - - - - - - - - - - - - - - - - -

_____

_____

- - - - - - - - - - - - - - - - - -

_____

Main Character

_____

- - - - - - - - - - - - - - - - - -

_____

_____

- - - - - - - - - - - - - - - - - -

_____

Why I Like It

_____

- - - - - - - - - - - - - - - - - -

_____

_____

- - - - - - - - - - - - - - - - - -

_____

Name: _____ Date: _____

My Best Day

....

Directions: Write about your best day. The questions will help you.

❶ How did you feel when you woke up?

_____

- -
_____

- -
_____

❷ What did you do after you got out of bed?

_____

- -
_____

- -
_____

❸ What was the first thing that made your day great?

_____

- -
_____

- -
_____

❹ What was the last thing that made your day great?

_____

- -
_____

- -
_____

Name: _____ **Date:** _____

My Funny Day

. . . .

Directions: Write about a funny day. The questions will help you.

❶ Where were you?

_____

_____

_____

_____

❷ Who was with you?

_____

_____

_____

_____

❸ What was the first thing that made your day funny?

_____

_____

_____

_____

❹ What was the second thing that made your day funny?

_____

_____

_____

_____

Name: _____ **Date:** _____

Writing Ideas

Directions: On a separate sheet of paper, try some of these ideas to help you be a better writer.

- Write an ad for a toy.

- Write a book of wishes.

- Write a cartoon book.

- Write a comic strip book.

- Write a favorite foods list.

- Write a grocery list for a cat or dog.

- Write a joke book.

- Write a new nursery rhyme.

- Write a riddle book.

- Write a song.

Name: _____   **Date:** _____

Ways to Better Writing

Directions: Write a story about a big cat and a little dog. Try these ideas on a separate sheet of paper

❶ Make a list of things that could be funny. A cat could chase a dog. A cat could steal a dog's bone.

❷ Draw the story first. Make it like a comic strip.

❸ Write the story.

❹ Make the words fun. You could use new words for *big* and *little*. New words for *big* are *giant*, *great*, and *large*. New words for *little* are *small*, *mini*, *petite*, and *tiny*.

❺ Have a friend read the story. What else would make it more fun?

Name: _____ Date: _____

Ways to Better Listening

Directions: It takes practice to be a good listener. Play these games with a partner.

Player One: Hide a timer in the room.

Player Two: Find the timer when it goes off.

Player One: Sit in a chair with your eyes closed.

Player Two: Make the sound of an animal.

Player One: Tell what the animal is.

Player One: Make noise with two sticks.

Player Two: March until the noise stops.

Player One: Say an action like, "Stand up."

Player Two: Do the opposite.

Name: _____ **Date:** _____

Ways to Better Speaking and Listening

Directions: It takes practice to be a good speaker and listener. Play these games with a partner.

Player One: Look around the room. Choose something to describe. Say one clue like, "I see something blue."

Player Two: Ask something like, "Is it the ball?"

Player One: Add one more clue if the guess is wrong.

Player Two: Guess again. Keep going until the thing is guessed.

Player One: Say, "I got on the bus. I brought a _____."

Player Two: Repeat the first sentence and add something new.

Player One: Keep adding to the list. Start over when the list is too long.

Name: _____ **Date:** _____

Count Them!

Directions: Write the missing numbers.

1		3		5
6			9	
	12	13		
			19	
21			24	

Name: _____ Date: _____

Count More!

Directions: Write the missing numbers.

26		28		
	32			35
		38		40
		43		
46				50

Name: _____ **Date:** _____

Count Even More!

Directions: Write the missing numbers.

51		**53**		**55**
	57			**60**
	62		**64**	
66			**69**	
	72		**74**	

Name: _____ **Date:** _____

Count to 100!

Directions: Write the missing numbers.

76			79	
	82		84	
	87			90
		93		95
	97			100

Name: _____ **Date:** _____

Keep Counting!

Directions: Count by ones from the first number.

6				

23				

87				

96				

13				

Name: _____ **Date:** _____

Don't Stop Counting!

Directions: Count by ones from the first number.

19				

34				

45				

11				

78				

Name: _____ **Date:** _____

Count Those Numbers!

Directions: Count by ones from the first number.

29				

74				

32				

0				

10				

Name: _____ **Date:** _____

Count by 10s!

Directions: Count by tens. Write the missing numbers.

10	20		40	

30		50		

60		80		

50				90

20	30			

Name: _____ Date: _____

Count More 10s!

Directions: Count by tens. Write the missing numbers.

0			30	

40		60		

30	40			70

50	60		80	

60				100

Name: _____ **Date:** _____

Keep Counting Those 10s!

Directions: Count by tens. Write the missing numbers.

0	10	20		

40			70	

10			40	50

20		40	50	

30			60	

Name: _____ Date: _____

More 10s to Count!

Directions: Count by tens. Write the missing numbers.

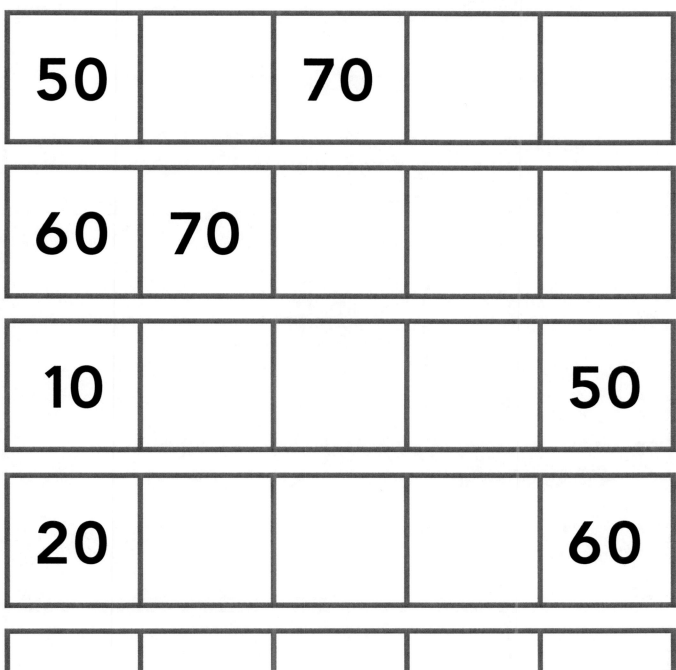

50		70		
60	70			
10				50
20				60
40	50			

Name: _____ **Date:** _____

How Many Dots?

Directions: Write the number.

1

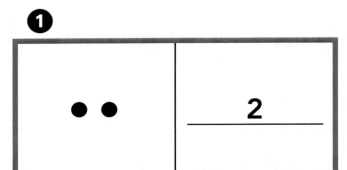

2

2

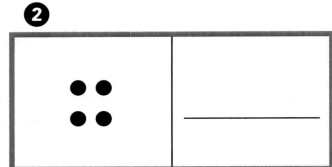

3

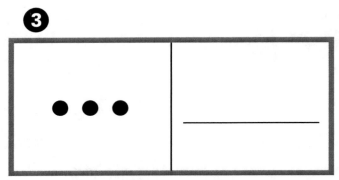

4

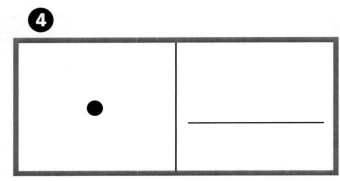

5

6

© Shell Education

Name: _____ Date: _____

How Many Apples?

Directions: Write the number.

1

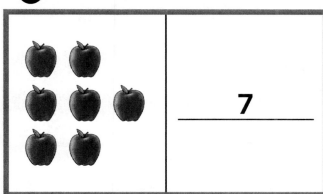

7

2

_____

3

_____

4

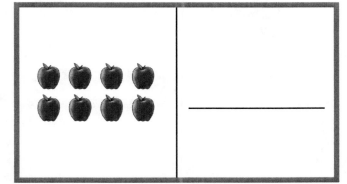

_____

5

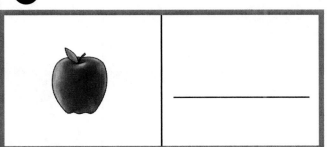

_____

6

_____

Name: _____ **Date:** _____

How Many Balls?

. . . .

Directions: Write the number.

1

 ___9___

2

 _____

3

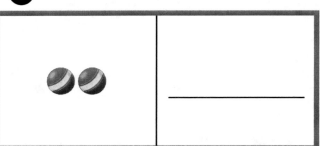 _____

4

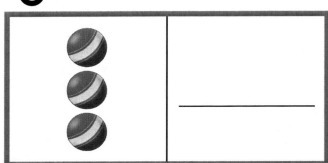 _____

5

_____

6

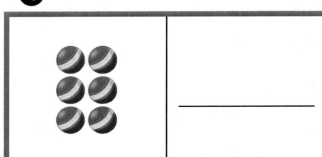 _____

Name: _____ **Date:** _____

How Many Hats?

Directions: Write the number.

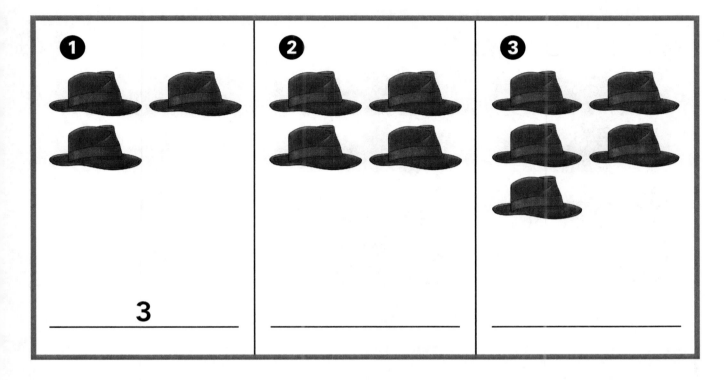

❶

3
_____

❷

_____

❸

_____

❹

_____

❺

_____

❻

_____

Name: _____ Date: _____

How Many Dogs?

Directions: Write the number.

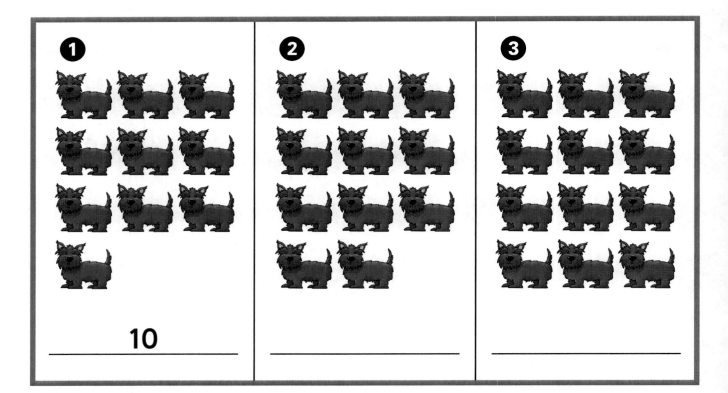

① _____ 10 _____

② _____

③ _____

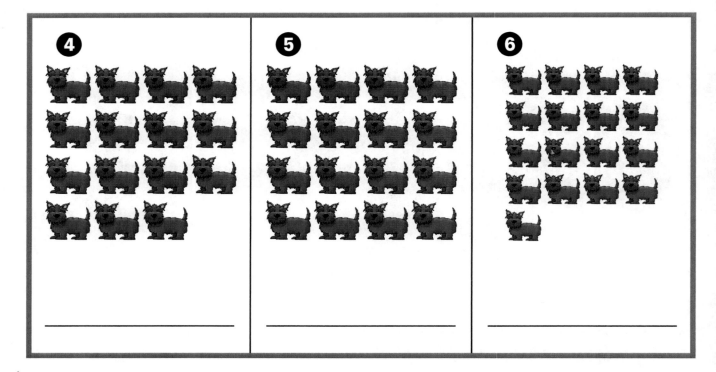

④ _____

⑤ _____

⑥ _____

Name: _____ Date: _____

How Many Cats?

Directions: Write the number.

1	2	3
1	_____	_____

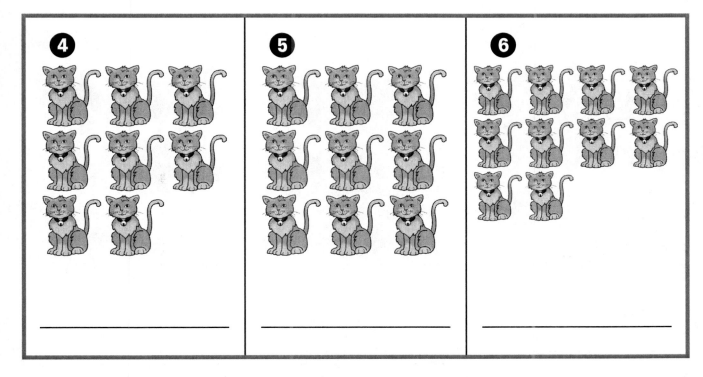

4	5	6
_____	_____	_____

Name: _____ Date: _____

How Many Balloons?

Directions: Write the number.

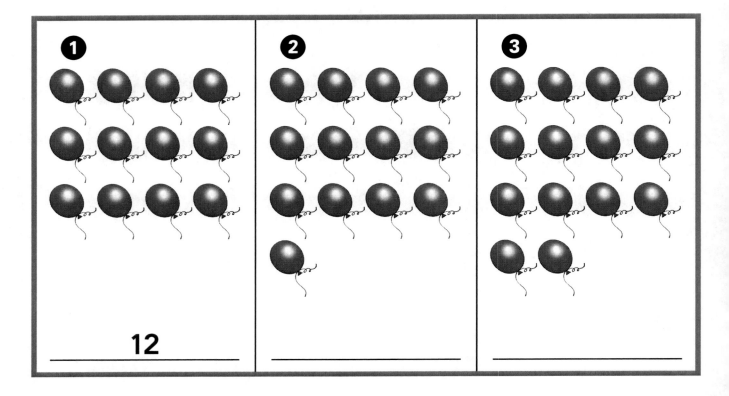

12

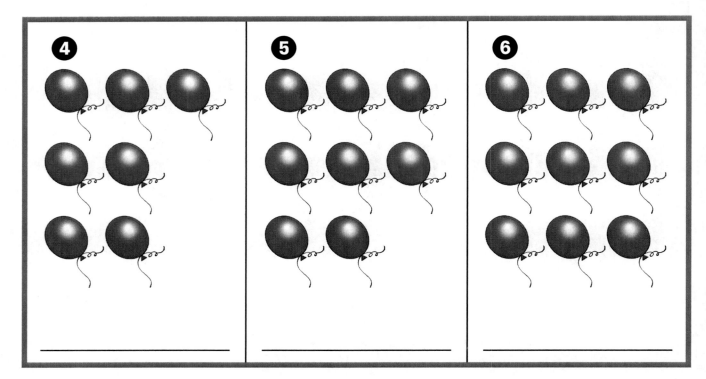

Name: _____ **Date:** _____

How Many Pencils?

Directions: Count the pencils. Then, answer the questions.

1

How many pencils? _____

2

How many pencils? _____

3

How many pencils? _____

4

How many pencils? _____

Name: _____ **Date:** _____

How Many Bugs?

....

Directions: Count the bugs. Then, answer the questions.

1

How many bugs? _____

2

How many bugs? _____

3

How many bugs? _____

4

How many bugs? _____

Name: _____ Date: _____

How Many Shoes?

Directions: Count the shoes. Then, answer the questions.

1

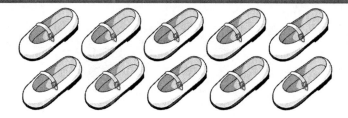

How many shoes? _____

2

How many shoes? _____

3

How many shoes? _____

4

How many shoes? _____

Name: _____ **Date:** _____

How Many Fish?

....

Directions: Count the fish. Then, answer the questions.

1

How many fish? _____

2

How many fish? _____

3

How many fish? _____

4

How many fish? _____

Name: _____ **Date:** _____

How Many Stars?

Directions: Count the stars. Then, answer the questions.

❶

How many stars? _____

❷

How many stars? _____

❸

How many stars? _____

Name: _____ **Date:** _____

How Many Shells?

....

Directions: Count the shells. Then, answer the questions.

①

How many shells? _____

②

How many shells? _____

③

How many shells? _____

 #50883—Bright & Brainy: Kindergarten Practice

Name: _____ **Date:** _____

How Many Birds?

Directions: Count the birds. Then, answer the questions.

1

How many birds? _____

2

How many birds? _____

3

How many birds? _____

Name: _____ **Date:** _____

How Many Nuts?

··

Directions: Count the nuts. Then, answer the questions.

❶

How many nuts? _____

❷

How many nuts? _____

❸

How many nuts? _____

Name: _____ Date: _____

Count Up the Suns!

Directions: Answer the questions.

1

Draw one more. How many? _____

2

Draw one more. How many? _____

3

Draw one more. How many? _____

4

Draw one more. How many? _____

Name: _____ Date: _____

Count Up the Apples!

Directions: Answer the questions.

1

Draw one more.
How many? _____

2

Draw one more.
How many? _____

3

Draw one more.
How many? _____

4

Draw one more.
How many? _____

Name: _____ **Date:** _____

Count Up the Cans!

Directions: Answer the questions.

❶

Draw one more. How many? _____

❷

Draw one more. How many? _____

❸

Draw one more. How many? _____

❹

Draw one more. How many? _____

Name: _____ **Date:** _____

Count Up the Bags!

Directions: Answer the questions.

1

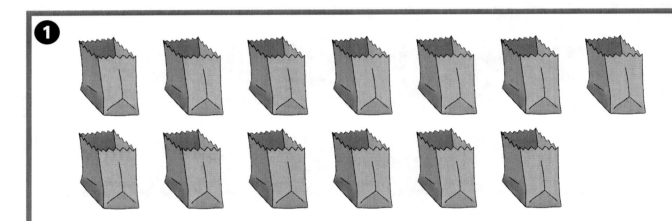

Draw one more.
How many? _____

2

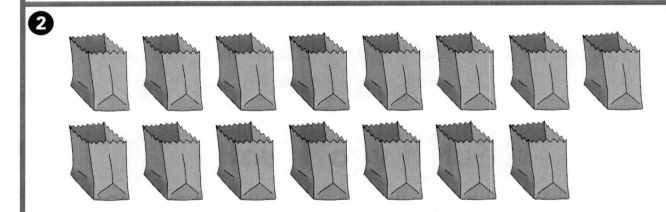

Draw one more.
How many? _____

Name: _____ **Date:** _____

Count Up the Cars!

Directions: Count the cars. Then, answer the questions.

1

How many cars? _____

2

How many cars? _____

3

How many cars? _____

4

How many cars? _____

#50883—*Bright & Brainy: Kindergarten Practice*

Name: _____ **Date:** _____

Count Up the Frogs!

Directions: Count the frogs. Then, answer the questions.

❶

How many frogs? _____

❷

How many frogs? _____

❸

How many frogs? _____

❹

How many frogs? _____

Name: _____ **Date:** _____

Count Up the Hens!

Directions: Count the hens. Then, answer the questions.

1

How many hens? _____

2

How many hens? _____

3

How many hens? _____

4

How many hens? _____

Name: _____ **Date:** _____

Count Up the Ants!

Directions: Count the ants. Then, answer the questions.

1

How many ants? _____

2

How many ants? _____

3

How many ants? _____

4

How many ants? _____

Name: _____ **Date:** _____

Count the Balls and Bats!

Directions: Count the balls and bats. Then, follow the steps.

1

How many balls? _____

Circle the bats that show the *same*.

2

How many balls? _____

Circle the bats that show the *same*.

Name: _____ **Date:** _____

Count the Shoes and Socks!

Directions: Count the socks and shoes. Then, follow the steps.

---

❶

How many socks? _____

Circle the shoes that show *less*.

---

❷

How many socks? _____

Circle the shoes that show *less*.

Name: _____ **Date:** _____

Count the Apples and Ants!

Directions: Count the apples and ants. Then, follow the steps.

1

How many apples? _____

Circle the ants that show *more*.

2

How many apples? _____

Circle the ants that show *more*.

Name: _____ **Date:** _____

Count the Suns and Caps!

Directions: Count the suns and caps. Then, follow the steps.

❶

How many suns are there? _____

Circle the caps that show *less*.

❷

How many suns are there? _____

Circle the caps that show *less*.

Name: _____ **Date:** _____

More or Less?

....

Directions: Look at the numbers on the boxes.
Then, follow the steps.

---

❶

| **2** | **3** |

Draw a circle around the box that has *more*.

Cross out the box that has *less*.

---

❷

| **8** | **0** |

Draw a circle around the box that has *more*.

Cross out the box that has *less*.

---

❸

| **7** | **8** |

Draw a circle around the box that has *more*.

Cross out the box that has *less*.

---

❹

| **6** | **5** |

Draw a circle around the box that has *more*.

Cross out the box that has *less*.

Name: _____ Date: _____

Is It More or Less?

Directions: Look at the numbers on the boxes. Then, follow the steps.

❶

| 6 | 9 |

Draw a circle around the box that has *less*.

Cross out the box that has *more*.

❷

| 8 | 0 |

Draw a circle around the box that has *more*.

Cross out the box that has *less* dogs.

❸

| 4 | 5 |

Draw a circle around the box that has *less*.

Cross out the box that has *more*.

❹

| 1 | 0 |

Draw a circle around the box that has *less*.

Cross out the box that has *more*.

Name: _____ Date: _____

Tell Which Box

Directions: Look at the numbers on the boxes.
Then, follow the steps.

①

| 10 | | 9 |

Draw a circle around the box that has *less*.

Cross out the box that has *more*.

②

| 9 | | 8 |

Draw a circle around the box that has *more*.

Cross out the box that has *less*.

③

| 9 | | 10 |

Draw a circle around the box that has *less*.

Cross out the box that has *more*.

④

| 11 | | 10 |

Draw a circle around the box that has *more*.

Cross out the box that has *less*.

Name: _____ **Date:** _____

Which Box?

Directions: Look at the numbers on the boxes. Then, follow the steps.

❶

| 7 | | 6 |

Cross out the box that has *more*.

Draw a circle around the box that has *less*.

❷

| 4 | | 3 |

Draw a circle around the box that has *more*.

Cross out the box that has *less*.

❸

| 5 | | 8 |

Cross out the box that has *more*.

Draw a circle around the box that has *less*.

❹

| 1 | | 0 |

Cross out the box that has *less*.

Draw a circle around the box that has *more*.

Name: _____ **Date:** _____

Add Up the Apples!

Directions: Add up the apples to solve the problems.

❶

$$2 \quad + \quad 1 \quad = \quad 3$$

❷

$$2 \quad + \quad 2 \quad = \quad \rule{3cm}{0.4pt}$$

❸

$$3 \quad + \quad 2 \quad = \quad \rule{3cm}{0.4pt}$$

❹

$$1 \quad + \quad 2 \quad = \quad \rule{3cm}{0.4pt}$$

Name: _____ **Date:** _____

Add Up the Eggs!

Directions: Add up the eggs to solve the problems.

1

4   +   1   =   5

2

1   +   1   =   _____

3

1   +   4   =   _____

4

3   +   2   =   _____

Name: _____ **Date:** _____

Count All of Those Bones!

Directions: Cross out bones to show the problem. Then, answer the questions.

❶ The dog has 3 bones.

He ate 2 bones.

How many bones are left? _____

❷ The dog has 4 bones.

He ate 2 bones.

How many bones are left? _____

❸ The dog has 5 bones.

He ate 3 bones.

How many bones are left? _____

Name: _____ **Date:** _____

Count All of Those Nuts!

Directions: Cross out the nuts to show the problem. Then, answer the questions.

❶ The squirrel has 6 nuts.

He ate 3 nuts.

How many nuts are left? _____

❷ The squirrel has 7 nuts.

He ate 4 nuts.

How many nuts are left? _____

❸ The squirrel has 7 nuts.

He ate 5 nuts.

How many nuts are left? _____

Name: _____ **Date:** _____

Count All of Those Stars!

Directions: Count the stars. Then, follow the steps.

❶

How many stars? _____

Draw 1 more. How many now? _____

❷

How many stars? _____

Draw 1 more. How many now? _____

❸

How many stars? _____

Draw 1 more. How many now? _____

Name: _____ **Date:** _____

Count All of Those Hats!

Directions: Count the hats. Then, follow the steps.

❶

How many hats? _____

Draw 2 more. How many now? _____

❷

How many hats? _____

Draw 3 more. How many now? _____

❸

How many hats? _____

Draw 4 more. How many now? _____

Name: _____ **Date:** _____

Count All of Those Balls!

Directions: Count the balls. Then, follow the steps.

❶

How many balls? _____

Draw 4 more. How many now? _____

❷

How many balls? _____

Draw 5 more. How many now? _____

❸

How many balls? _____

Draw 2 more. How many now? _____

#50883—Bright & Brainy: Kindergarten Practice

Name: _____ **Date:** _____

Counting Bones!

....

Directions: Count the bones. Then, follow the steps.

1

How many bones? _____

Draw 1 more. How many now? _____

2

How many bones? _____

Draw 8 more. How many now? _____

3

How many bones? _____

Draw 3 more. How many now? _____

 #50883—Bright & Brainy: Kindergarten Practice

Name: _____ **Date:** _____

Take Away Some Apples!

Directions: Count the apples. Then, follow the steps.

1

How many apples? _____

Cross out 1. How many are left? _____

2

How many apples? _____

Cross out 2. How many are left? _____

3

How many apples? _____

Cross out 3. How many are left? _____

Name: _____ **Date:** _____

Take Away Some Bats!

Directions: Count the bats. Then, follow the steps.

1

How many bats? _____

Cross out 3. How many are left? _____

2

How many bats? _____

Cross out 5. How many are left? _____

3

How many bats? _____

Cross out 4. How many are left? _____

Name: _____ **Date:** _____

Take Away Some Dogs!

Directions: Count the dogs. Then, follow the steps.

❶

How many dogs? _____

Cross out 2. How many are left? _____

❷

How many dogs? _____

Cross out 1. How many are left? _____

❸

How many dogs? _____

Cross out 5. How many are left? _____

Name: _____ **Date:** _____

Take Away Some Cats!

Directions: Count the cats. Then, follow the steps.

1

How many cats? _____

Cross out 3. How many are left? _____

2

How many cats? _____

Cross out 3. How many are left? _____

3

How many cats? _____

Cross out 0. How many are left? _____

Name: _____ Date: _____

Work with Numbers

Directions: Follow the steps below.

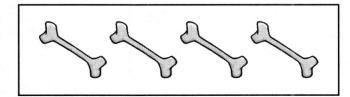   

_____ **+** _____ **=** _____
  bones   bones   bones

❶ How many bones are in the first box? Write the number on the first line.

❷ Draw 1 bone in the other box. Write the number on the second line.

❸ How many bones are there in all? Write the number on the last line.

Name: _____ **Date:** _____

Work with More Numbers

. . . .

Directions: Draw more hats. Then, solve each problem.

 1

Draw 2 hats.

_____ **+** _____ **=** _____
hats   hats   hats

2

Draw 3 hats.

_____ **+** _____ **=** _____
hats   hats   hats

Name: _____ Date: _____

Add Some Logs

Directions: Draw more logs. Then, solve each problem.

1

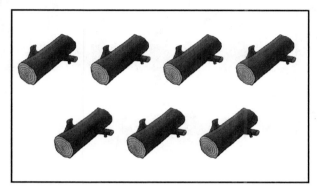

Draw 1 log.

_____ **+** _____ **=** _____
   logs   log   logs

2

Draw 2 logs.

_____ **+** _____ **=** _____
   logs   logs   logs

Name: _____ **Date:** _____

Find 10 Eggs

Directions: Draw more eggs. Then, solve each problem.

 1

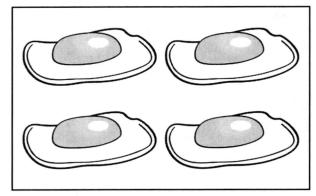

Draw 2 logs.

_____ **+** _____ **=** _____

eggs   eggs   eggs

2

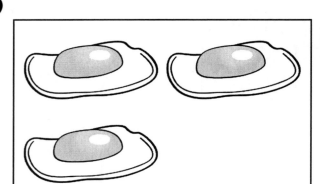

Draw 3 eggs.

_____ **+** _____ **=** _____

eggs   eggs   eggs

Name: _____ **Date:** _____

What's the Problem?

Directions: Write the answer to each problem.

1 ☀ ☀ + ☀ = __3__ suns

2 ☀ ☀ ☀ + ☀ ☀ = _____ suns

3 ☀ + ☀ ☀ ☀ ☀ = _____ suns

4 ☀ ☀ + ☀ ☀ = _____ suns

5 ☀ + ☀ ☀ ☀ = _____ suns

Name: _____ Date: _____

Finish the Problems

Directions: Follow the steps to solve each problem.

①

_____ - _____ = _____

Cross out 1 star. How many stars are left?

②

_____ - _____ = _____

Cross out 2 stars. How many stars are left?

③

_____ - _____ = _____

Cross out 3 stars. How many stars are left?

Name: _____ **Date:** _____

Big Problems with Bugs!

Directions: Count the bugs in the first box and second box. Write the numbers. Then, add the bugs.

1

_____ **+** _____ **=** _____

2

_____ **+** _____ **=** _____

3

_____ **+** _____ **=** _____

4

_____ **+** _____ **=** _____

Name: _____ **Date:** _____

Big Problems with Ants!

Directions: Count the ants in the first box and second box. Write the numbers. Then, add the ants.

1

_____ **+** _____ **=** _____

2

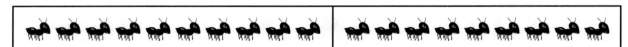

_____ **+** _____ **=** _____

3

_____ **+** _____ **=** _____

4

_____ **+** _____ **=** _____

Name: _____ **Date:** _____

Measure Up!

Directions: Measure the items below with pencils.

Items to measure	Length with pencils
1 	_____ **pencils**
2 2 + 2 = 4 + 3 = 7 + 3 = a b c d e f g	_____ **pencils**
3	_____ **pencil**

Name: _____ **Date:** _____

Measure and Compare

Directions: Find the items below. Measure the items with your finger. Have a friend do the same thing.

Items to measure	Length with my fingers	Length with my friend's fingers
	_____ fingers	_____ fingers
	_____ fingers	_____ fingers
	_____ fingers	_____ fingers

Name: _____ Date: _____

Measure and Compare More

Directions: Measure the items below with paper clips.

Items to measure	Length with paper clips
$2 + 2 =$ $4 + 3 =$ $7 + 3 =$ a b c d e f g	_____ paper clips
	_____ paper clips
	_____ paper clips

Name: _____ **Date:** _____

Measure and Compare Big Things

Directions: Find these items. Measure the items with your hand. Have a friend do the same thing.

Items to measure	Length with my hands	Length with my friend's hands
	_____ hands	_____ hands
	_____ hands	_____ hands
	_____ hands	_____ hands

Name: _____ Date: _____

Sort and Count!

Directions: Answer the questions.

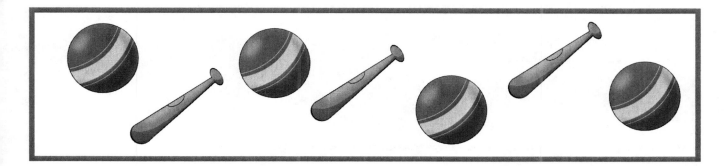

❶ Count the balls. How many? _____

❷ Count the bats. How many? _____

❸ Count the suns. How many? _____

❹ Count the clouds. How many? _____

Name: _____ Date: _____

Sort and Count More!

Directions: Answer the questions.

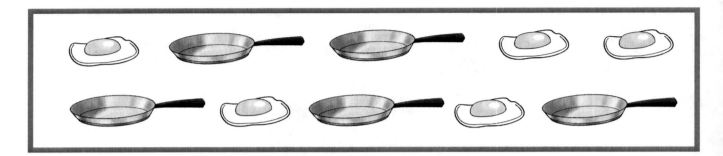

1 Count the pans. How many? _____

2 Count the eggs. How many? _____

3 Count the stars. How many? _____

4 Count the moons. How many? _____

Name: _____ Date: _____

Sort and Count by Size

Directions: Answer the questions.

1 Count the little cars. How many? _____

2 Count the big cars. How many? _____

3 Count the big dogs. How many? _____

4 Count the little dogs. How many? _____

Name: _____ **Date:** _____

Sort and Count by Shape

Directions: Answer the questions.

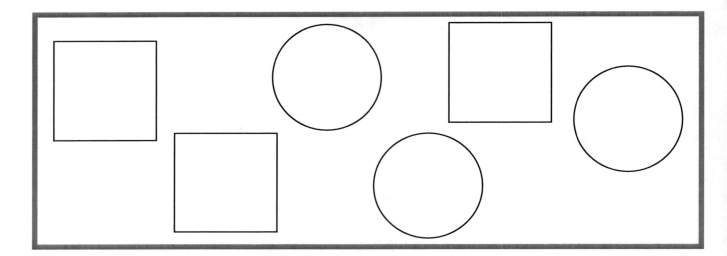

❶ Count the circles. How many? _____

❷ Count the squares. How many? _____

❸ Count the food things. How many? _____

❹ Count the play things. How many? _____

Name: _____ **Date:** _____

Find the Shapes

Directions: Look at the picture. Then, answer the questions.

❶ What shape is the sign?

   a. square

   b. rectangle

   c. circle

❷ Where is the man?

   a. above the car

   b. next to the car

   c. under the car

❸ What shape is the cash?

   a. square

   b. rectangle

   c. circle

❹ Where is the cloud?

   a. in front of the car

   b. above the car

   c. under the car

Name: _____ **Date:** _____

Find More Shapes

. . . .

Directions: Look at the picture. Then, answer the questions.

① **What shape is the art?**

   a. square

   b. rectangle

   c. circle

② **What shape is the rug?**

   a. circle

   b. rectangle

   c. square

③ **Where is the rug?**

   a. above the bed

   b. behind the bed

   c. under the bed

④ **Where is the art?**

   a. on the floor

   b. on the wall

   c. on the bed

Name: _____ Date: _____

Where Are the Shapes?

Directions: Look at the picture. Then, answer the questions.

❶ **What shape are the windows?**

　a.　square

　b.　rectangle

　c.　circle

❷ **What shape is the door?**

　a.　circle

　b.　rectangle

　c.　square

❸ **Where is the grass?**

　a.　above the house

　b.　in front of the house

　c.　on the door

❹ **Where is the door?**

　a.　on the top of the house

　b.　under the house

　c.　by a window

Name: _____ **Date:** _____

Make the Shapes

....

Directions: Read all the steps. Then, do each step.

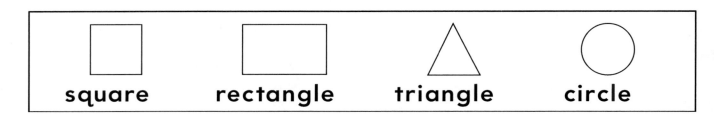

| square | rectangle | triangle | circle |

❶ Draw a square at the bottom of the box.

❷ Draw a circle inside the square.

❸ Draw a rectangle above the square.

❹ Draw a triangle on each side of the square.

Name: _____ **Date:** _____

Name the Shapes

Directions: Draw a line from each shape to its name.

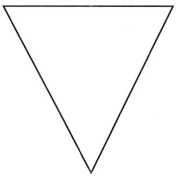

square

rectangle

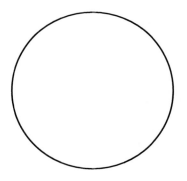

circle

triangle

Name: _____ **Date:** _____

Shape Match

Directions: Draw a line from each shape to its name.

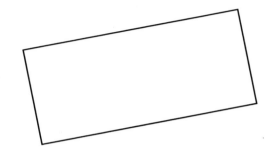

square

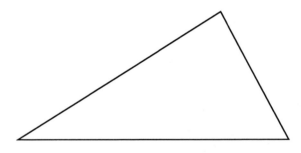

rectangle

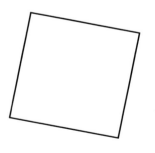

circle

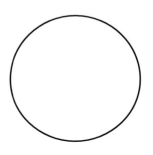

triangle

Name: _____ **Date:** _____

More Shape Naming

Directions: Color the squares red. Color the triangles green. Color the circles blue. Color the rectangles yellow.

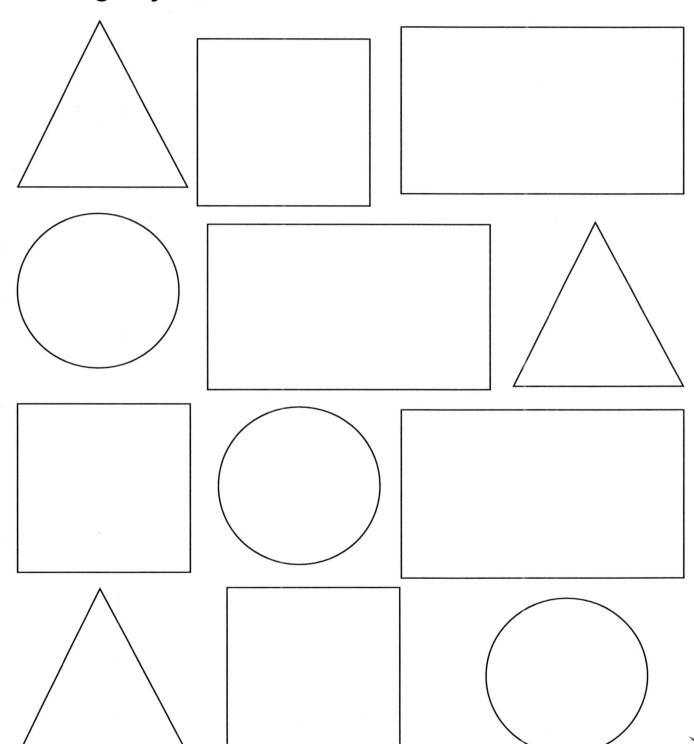

Name: _____ **Date:** _____

Build with Shapes

....

Directions: Follow the steps.

❶ Outline the star in yellow.

❷ Outline the triangles in green.

❸ Outline the rectangles in black.

❹ Outline the squares in blue.

❺ Outline the circle in red.

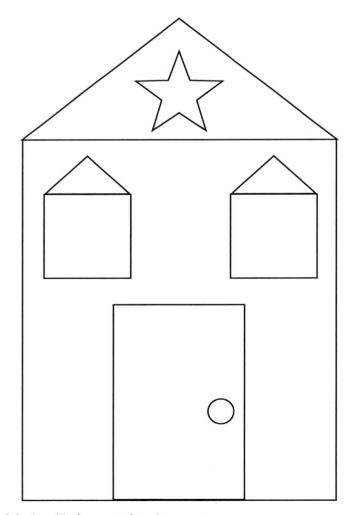

Name: _____ **Date:** _____

Flat or Solid?

Directions: Write *solid* under the solid figures.
Write *flat* under the flat figures.

These figures are flat:	These figures are solid.
triangle square rectangle circle	cube rectangular prism sphere

1

_____

2

_____

3

_____

4

_____

5

_____

6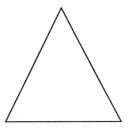

_____

Name: _____ **Date:** _____

Flat and Solid Figures

Directions: Write *solid* under the solid figures.
Write *flat* under the flat figures.

These figures are flat:	These figures are solid.
triangle square rectangle circle	 cube rectangular prism sphere

1

_____

2

_____

3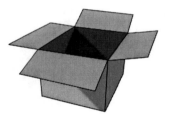

_____

4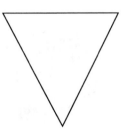

_____

5

_____

6

_____

Name: _____ Date: _____

How Many Sides?

Directions: Count the sides. Write a number by each side.

1

How many sides? _____

2

How many sides? _____

3

How many sides? _____

Name: _____ **Date:** _____

Count the Sides

∙∙

Directions: Count the sides. Write a number by each side.

How many sides? _____

  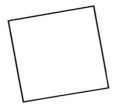

How many sides? _____

How many sides? _____

 #50883—Bright & Brainy: Kindergarten Practice

Name: _____ **Date:** _____

Count More Sides

Directions: Count the sides. Write a number by each side.

 1

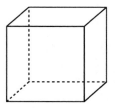

How many sides? _____

2

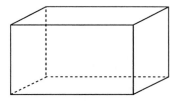

How many sides? _____

3

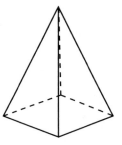

How many sides? _____

Name: _____ **Date:** _____

Count All the Sides

Directions: Answer the questions.

These figures are flat:	These figures are solid.
 square rectangle triangle	cube rectangular prism pyramid

❶ How many sides does a square have? _____

❷ How many sides does a cube have? _____

❸ How many sides does a rectangle have? _____

❹ How many sides does a rectangular prism

have? _____

❺ How many sides does a triangle have? _____

❻ How many sides does a pyramid have? _____

Name: _____ **Date:** _____

Alike and Different Shapes

Directions: Answer the questions.

❶ How are these figures alike?

_____

- -

_____

_____

- -

_____

❷ How are these figures different?

_____

- -

_____

_____

- -

_____

Name: _____ **Date:** _____

More Alike and Different Shapes

Directions: Answer the questions.

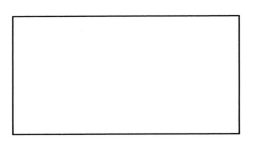 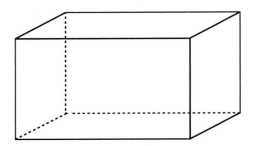

❶ How are these figures alike?

_____

_ _

_____

_ _

_____

❷ How are these figures different?

_____

_ _

_____

_ _

_____

Name: _____ Date: _____

Make Flat Shapes

Directions: Trace each shape.

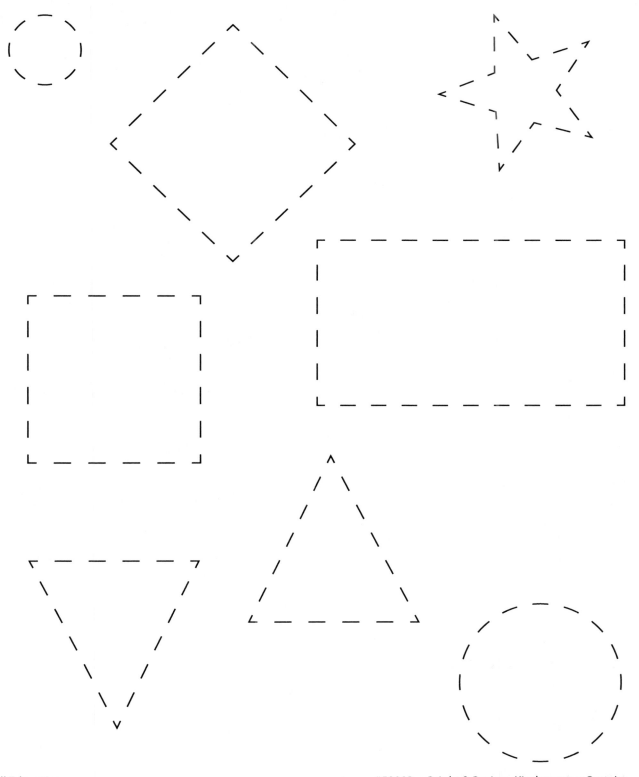

References Cited

Annis, L. F., and D. B Annis. 1987. *Does practice make perfect? The effects of repetition on student learning.* Paper presented at the annual meeting of the American Educational Research Association, Washington, DC.

Marzano, R. 2010. When practice makes perfect...sense. *Educational Leadership* 68:81–83.

National Governors Association Center for Best Practices and Council of Chief State School Officers. 2010. Common core standards. http://www.corestandards.org/the-standards.

Answer Key

Draw the Line (page 11)
1. Students should have drawn lines through the airplane images.
2. Students should have drawn lines through the can images.
3. Students should have drawn lines through the ball images.
4. Students should have drawn lines through the dad images.

Follow These! (page 12)
1. Students should have drawn lines through the bus images.
2. Students should have drawn lines through the hen images.
3. Students should have drawn lines through the pen images.
4. Students should have drawn lines through the star images.

Is It the Same? (page 13)
1. Students should have drawn lines through the bed images.
2. Students should have drawn lines through the boat images.
3. Students should have drawn lines through the book images.
4. Students should have drawn lines through the pencil images.

Find the Same Pictures (page 14)
1. Students should have drawn lines through the bag images.
2. Students should have drawn lines through the bat images.
3. Students should have drawn lines through the brush images.
4. Students should have drawn lines through the cat images.

Missing Words! (page 15)
1. can
2. car
3. dad
4. bee

Which Word? (page 16)
1. bed
2. hat
3. cat
4. box

Write It Right (page 17)
1. This is a baby.
2. This is a duck.
3. This is a shoe.

Write More (page 18)
1. This is a bear.
2. This is a book.
3. This is a shoe.

Lowercase Letter Match (page 19)
Students' responses will vary.

More Lowercase Letter Match (page 21)
Students' responses will vary.

Capital Letter Match (page 23)
Students' responses will vary.

More Capital Letter Match (page 25)
Students' responses will vary.

Rhyme Time (page 27)
1. pan
2. man
3. jar
4. rock

Answer Key *(cont.)*

More Rhyme Time (page 28)
1. fox
2. star
3. box
4. wig

Find the Rhyme (page 29)
1. rain
2. bed
3. goat
4. cat

Find These Rhymes (page 30)
1. snail
2. man
3. knee
4. dog

How Many Parts? (page 31)
1. 1
2. 2
3. 1
4. 1
5. 1
6. 2

What Is That Sound? (page 32)
1. ball, bed
2. cat, can
3. dog
4. fan, fox

Name That Letter Sound (page 33)
1. kite, key
2. leaf, leg
3. mop, milk
4. nose, nest, net

Name More Letter Sounds (page 34)
1. sun, scissors
2. turtle
3. vest
4. whale, wig

Beginning Sounds (page 35)
1. h; hat
2. j; jar
3. c; can
4. f; fan
5. b; bed
6. s; sun

More Beginning Sounds (page 36)
1. d; dog
2. b; box
3. p; pen
4. h; hen
5. p; pig
6. b; block

Even More Beginning Sounds (page 37)
1. b; boat
2. c; cake
3. l; lock
4. b; bell
5. c; cat
6. n; nose

Make New Words! (page 38)
1. lock
2. arm
3. top
4. rain

What Sound? (page 39)
1. b
2. p
3. s
4. c

Missing Letter (page 40)
1. a
2. o
3. a
4. e

Answer Key *(cont.)*

Word Endings (page 41)

1. t
2. n
3. g
4. d

New Words (page 42)

1. mop
2. cat
3. can
4. man

More New Words (page 43)

1. pen
2. pig
3. goat
4. car

Name That Short Vowel (page 44)

can, map, hat

Name More Short Vowels (page 45)

wig, mitt

Can You Name That Short Vowel? (page 46)

duck, sun, bug

Name That Long Vowel (page 47)

rain, snake, cake

Name More Long Vowels (page 48)

lion, ice cream, tie

Can You Name These Long Vowels? (page 49)

shoe, balloon

Read Tricky Words (page 50)

1. have
2. I
3. like
4. are

Find the Right Word (page 51)

1. Do
2. have
3. is
4. with

Read Even More Tricky Words (page 52)

1. The
2. Do
3. They
4. He

Use Tricky Words (page 53)

1. was
2. for
3. not
4. that

Spell Tricky Words (page 54)

1. saw
2. cat
3. big
4. had

Spell More Tricky Words (page 55)

1. have
2. is
3. Her
4. want

Choose the Tricky Word (page 56)

1. went
2. saw
3. was
4. like

Answer Key (cont.)

Choose More Tricky Words (page 57)

1. Look
2. fun
3. looks
4. too

Practice Your Letters (page 58)

Students should have traced the letters correctly.

Practice More Letters (page 59)

Students should have traced the letters correctly.

Practice Even More Letters (page 60)

Students should have traced the letters correctly.

Lots of Letters (page 61)

Students should have traced the letters correctly.

Trace More Letters (page 62)

Students should have traced the letters correctly.

Keep Tracing (page 63)

Students should have traced the letters correctly.

Which Word Is Right? (page 64)

1. bat
2. can
3. Dad
4. Mom

Choose the Right Word (page 65)

1. dog
2. baby
3. bird
4. bus

Which Word? (page 66)

1. hen
2. pen
3. house
4. book

Choose More Words (page 67)

1. ant
2. dish
3. nest
4. tub

Finish the Sentence (page 68)

1. flaps
2. wags
3. swims
4. hops

What Do These Pictures Say? (page 69)

1. rides
2. runs
3. naps
4. reads

Read Carefully! (page 70)

1. moves
2. skips
3. stops
4. flies

Read These Carefully! (page 71)

1. plays
2. hugs
3. draws
4. rests

One or Two? (page 72)

1. pig
2. hats
3. pans
4. sun

Answer Key (cont.)

More Than One? (page 73)
1. bed
2. apples
3. can
4. nuts

How Many in These? (page 74)
1. foxes
2. watches
3. bone
4. brush

More Plural Practice (page 75)
1. tree
2. sock
3. locks
4. coat

Finish the Questions (page 76)
1. What
2. Who
3. What
4. Who

Finish More Questions (page 77)
1. Where
2. Who
3. Who
4. Where

Where Is It? (page 78)
1. on
2. by
3. on
4. by

Where Are They? (page 79)
1. in
2. by
3. by
4. in

Capital Mistake (page 80)
1. i have a dog.
2. my dog has spots.
3. May i pet your dog?
4. your dog is big!

Capitalize It (page 81)
I, They, I, Max, He, She

Punctuate the Sentences (page 82)
1. ?
2. !
3. .
4. ?

Punctuate More Sentences (page 83)
Suggested punctuation: Do you know how to snap? I do. It can be hard. I like to snap!

Name the Short Vowels (page 84)
1. a
2. o
3. a
4. e

Name More Short Vowels (page 85)
1. a
2. i
3. u
4. o

Spelling Fun (page 86)
1. car
2. sun
3. leg
4. cap

Answer Key (cont.)

More Spelling Words (page 87)
1. egg
2. pig
3. can
4. dad or man

Keep Spelling! (page 88)
1. cap
2. pan
3. wig
4. ham

Keep Spelling More Words! (page 89)
1. foot
2. ball
4. ring
5. duck

Ben the Elephant (page 90)
1. Ben
2. grass
3. trunk
4. trunk

Pal the Dog (page 91)
1. dog
2. the door
3. Pete's shoes
4. He helps Pete a lot.

Ducks! (page 92)
1. hen
2. a nest
3. 4 weeks
4. ducklings

Frogs Are Neat (page 93)
1. tadpole
2. **in** the water
3. **uses its** tail
4. **in** the water

The Big Idea (page 94)
a

What's the Big Idea? (page 95)
b

Another Big Idea (page 96)
c

Help the Author (page 97)
a

Give the Story a Title (page 98)
b

Give This Story a Title (page 99)
c

Tell About the Picture (page 100)
1. The cat has yarn.
2. The dog has a bone.
3. The kids look at the bell.

What Does the Picture Tell? (page 101)
1. The girls smile.
2. Dad has a bag.
3. The boy takes a drink.

What Does the Picture Show? (page 102)
1. Jan pats her desk.
2. Bob is on a stage.
3. Niko walks home.

Tell About these Pictures (page 103)
1. José swims! He is happy!
2. Jim tip toes.
3. Sara rides her bike.

Tom's Story (page 104)
Bats can fly fast, sleep upside down, and catch bugs in the air.

Pat's Story (page 105)
Mice can run up walls, have long tails, can do tricks, and nap in boxes.

Answer Key *(cont.)*

Be a Sentence Detective (page 106)

1. Students should have circled the image of the duck quacking.
2. Students should have circled the image of the brush on the table.
3. Students should have circled the image of the girl using a fan.
4. Students should have circled the image of the fish in a pan.

Detect More Meanings (page 107)

1. Students should have circled the image of the key in a lock.
2. Students should have circled the image of the dad painting a bird house.
3. Students should have circled the image of the boy holding a puppy.
4. Students should have circled the image of the dad raking the grass.

Detect Even More Meanings (page 108)

1. Students should have circled the image of the pig in the pen.
2. Students should have circled the image of the hand ringing the bell.
3. Students should have circled the image of the man sawing a log.
4. Students should have circled the image of the girl ice skating.

Figure It Out (page 109)

1. Image of a boy with a sled at the top of a hill is circled.
2. Image of boy tying his shoe is circled.
3. Image of baby playing with a top is circled.
4. Image of a bowl is circled.

Prefix Practice (page 110)

1. unpin; a
2. unfair; a.
3. unbox; a
4. untie; a

More Prefix Practice (page 111)

1. redo
2. reglue
3. refill
4. reheat

Practice with Pre- (page 112)

1. Prechill
2. Prewash
3. Preheat
4. precut

Suffix Practice (page 113)

1. skillful
2. careful
3. playful
4. helpful

Show the Past (page 114)

1. worked
2. mixed
3. pulled
4. stayed

Sort the Words (page 115)

duck, *goat*, and *pig* should be connected to the barn with lines. *baby*, *man*, and *woman* should be connected to the house with lines.

Sort More Words (page 116)

bus and *car* should be connected to the wheels with lines. *apple*, *milk*, *nut*, and *peas* should be connected to the plate with lines.

Keep Sorting! (page 117)

red, *black*, and *orange* should be connected to the crayon with lines. *square*, *circle*, and *triangle* should be connected to the box with lines.

Answer Key (cont.)

Opposites (page 118)

1. line from *light* to paper; line from *heavy* to rock
2. line from *happy* to happy girl; line from *sad* to crying girl
3. line from *big* to big ball; line from *little* to little ball
4. line from *new* to new shoe; line from *old* to old shoe

More Opposites (page 119)

1. line from *down* to kite on ground; line from *up* to kite in air
2. line from *fat* to fat cat; line from *thin* to thin cat
3. line from *asleep* to child asleep; line from *awake* to child awake
4. line from *cold* to cup of ice water; line from *hot* to sun

Inside or Outside? (page 120)

bed, *dresser*, and *lamp* should be connected to the inside with lines. *tree*, *sun*, and *grass* should be connected to the outside with lines.

Farm or School? (page 121)

desk, *book*, and *crayon* should be connected to the school with lines. *hen*, *horse*, and *cow* should be connected to the barn with lines.

Your Body (page 122)

Check for lines drawn to the appropriate places on the body.

What's the Answer? (page 123)

1. a
2. b
3. a
4. c

Find the Answers (page 124)

1. c
2. c
3. a
4. a

Questions to Answer (page 125)

1. b
2. c
3. b
4. b

Read the Answer (page 126)

1. b
2. c
3. b
4. a

Book Log (page 127)

Students' responses will vary.

Opposite Characters (page 128)

Students' responses will vary.

Be a Great Reader! (page 129)

Students' responses will vary.

More Tips for Being a Great Reader (page 130)

Students' responses will vary.

My Good Book! (page 131)

Students' responses will vary.

My Book Review (page 132)

Students' responses will vary.

About a Pet (page 133)

Students' responses will vary.

My Review (page 134)

Students' responses will vary.

My Best Day (page 135)

Students' responses will vary.

My Funny Day (page 136)

Students' responses will vary.

Writing Ideas (page 137)

Students' responses will vary.

Ways to Better Writing (page 138)

Students' responses will vary.

Ways to Better Listening (page 139)

Students' responses will vary.

Ways to Better Speaking and Listening (page 140)

Students' responses will vary.

Count Them! (page 141)

Missing numbers are the following:

2, 4, 7, 8, 10, 11, 14, 15, 16, 17, 18, 20, 22, 23, 25

Count More! (page 142)

Missing numbers are the following:

27, 29, 30, 31, 33, 34, 36, 37, 39, 41, 42, 44, 45, 47, 48, 49

Count Even More! (page 143)

Missing numbers are the following:

52, 54, 56, 58, 59, 61, 63, 65, 67, 68, 70, 71, 73, 75

Count to 100! (page 144)

Missing numbers are the following:

77, 78, 80, 81, 83, 85, 86, 88, 89, 91, 92, 94, 96, 98, 99

Keep Counting! (page 145)

6	7	8	9	10
23	24	25	26	27
87	88	89	90	91
96	97	98	99	100
13	14	15	16	17

Don't Stop Counting! (page 146)

19	20	21	22	23
34	35	36	37	38
45	46	47	48	49
11	12	13	14	15
78	79	80	81	82

Count Those Numbers! (page 147)

29	30	31	32	33
74	75	76	77	78
32	33	34	35	36
0	1	2	3	4
10	11	12	13	14

Count by 10s! (page 148)

10	20	30	40	50
30	40	50	60	70
60	70	80	90	100
50	60	70	80	90
20	30	40	50	60

Answer Key (cont.)

Count More 10s! (page 149)

0	10	20	30	40

40	50	60	70	80

30	40	50	60	70

50	60	70	80	90

60	70	80	90	100

Keep Counting Those 10s! (page 150)

0	10	20	30	40

40	50	60	70	80

10	20	30	40	50

20	30	40	50	60

30	40	50	60	70

More 10s to Count! (page 151)

50	60	70	80	90

60	70	80	90	100

10	20	30	40	50

20	30	40	50	60

40	50	60	70	80

How Many Dots? (page 152)

1. 2
2. 4
3. 3
4. 1
5. 0
6. 5

How Many Apples? (page 153)

1. 7
2. 10
3. 6
4. 8
5. 1
6. 4

How Many Balls? (page 154)

1. 9
2. 8
3. 3
4. 6
5. 2
6. 1

How Many Hats? (page 155)

1. 3
2. 4
3. 5
4. 6
5. 7
6. 8

Answer Key (cont.)

How Many Dogs? (page 156)
1. 10
2. 11
3. 12
4. 15
5. 16
6. 17

How Many Cats? (page 157)
1. 1
2. 2
3. 3
4. 8
5. 9
6. 10

How Many Balloons? (page 158)
1. 12
2. 13
3. 14
4. 7
5. 8
6. 9

How Many Pencils? (page 159)
1. 4 pencils
2. 6 pencils
3. 8 pencils
4. 5 pencils

How Many Bugs? (page 160)
1. 3 bugs
2. 7 bugs
3. 2 bugs
4. 9 bugs

How Many Shoes? (page 161)
1. 10 shoes
2. 11 shoes
3. 7 shoes
4. 9 shoes

How Many Fish? (page 162)
1. 4 fish
2. 11 fish
3. 9 fish
4. 7 fish

How Many Stars? (page 163)
1. 5
2. 5
3. 5

How Many Shells? (page 164)
1. 6
2. 6
3. 6

How Many Birds? (page 165)
1. 8
2. 8
3. 8

How Many Nuts? (page 166)
1. 9
2. 9
3. 10

Count Up the Suns! (page 167)
1. 3 suns
2. 6 suns
3. 8 suns
4. 4 suns

Answer Key (cont.)

Count Up the Apples! (page 168)
1. 9 apples
2. 7 apples
3. 10 apples
4. 5 apples

Count Up the Cans! (page 169)
1. 9 cans
2. 7 cans
3. 5 cans
4. 11 cans

Count Up the Bags! (page 170)
1. 14 bags
2. 16 bags

Count Up the Cars! (page 171)
1. 6 cars
2. 4 cars
3. 3 cars
4. 5 cars

Count Up the Frogs! (page 172)
1. 3 frogs
2. 2 frogs
3. 7 frogs
4. 11 frogs

Count Up the Hens! (page 173)
1. 4 hens
2. 6 hens
3. 13 hens
4. 10 hens

Count Up the Ants! (page 174)
1. 5 ants
2. 11 ants
3. 9 ants
4. 6 ants

Count the Balls and Bats! (page 175)
1. 3; third box
2. 4; first box

Count the Shoes and Socks! (page 176)
1. 5; first box
2. 6; third box

Count the Apples and Ants! (page 177)
1. 8; first box
2. 6; third box

Count the Suns and Caps! (page 178)
1. 10; second box
2. 12; second box

More or Less? (page 179)
1. circle "3 box"; cross out "2 box"
2. circle "8 box"; cross out "0 box"
3. circle "8 box"; cross out "7 box"
4. circle around "6 box"; cross out "5 box"

Is It More or Less? (page 180)
1. circle "6 box"; cross out "9 box"
2. circle "8 box"; cross out "0 box"
3. circle "4 box"; cross out "5 box"
4. circle "0 box"; cross out "1 box"

Tell Which Box (page 181)
1. circle "9 box"; cross out "10 box"
2. circle "9 box"; cross out "8 box"
3. circle "9 box"; cross out "10 box"
4. circle out "11 box"; cross out "10 box"

Which Box? (page 182)
1. cross out "7 box"; circle "6 box"
2. circle "4 box"; cross out "3 box"
3. cross out "8 box"; circle "5 box"
4. cross out "0 box"; circle "1 box"

Answer Key *(cont.)*

Add Up the Apples! (page 183)
1. 3 apples
2. 4 apples
3. 5 apples
4. 3 apples

Add Up the Eggs! (page 184)
1. 5 eggs
2. 2 eggs
3. 5 eggs
4. 5 eggs

Count All of Those Bones! (page 185)
1. 1 bone
2. 2 bones
3. 2 bones

Count All of Those Nuts! (page 186)
1. 3 nuts
2. 3 nuts
3. 2 nuts

Count All of Those Stars! (page 187)
1. 3; 4
2. 5; 6
3. 4; 5

Count All of Those Hats! (page 188)
1. 6; 8
2. 6; 9
3. 4; 8

Count All of Those Balls! (page 189)
1. 3; 7
2. 4; 9
3. 7; 9

Counting Bones! (page 190)
1. 9; 10
2. 1; 9
3. 7; 10

Take Away Some Apples! (page 191)
1. 6; 5
2. 8; 6
3. 4; 1

Take Away Some Bats! (page 192)
1. 7; 4
2. 9; 4
3. 8; 4

Take Away Some Dogs! (page 193)
1. 8; 6
2. 9; 8
3. 8; 3

Take Away Some Cats! (page 194)
1. 10; 7
2. 9; 6
3. 7; 7

Work with Numbers (page 195)
$4 + 1 = 5$

Work with More Numbers (page 196)
$6 + 2 = 8$
$5 + 2 = 7$

Add Some Logs (page 197)
$7 + 1 = 8$
$2 + 2 = 4$

Answer Key (cont.)

Add Some Eggs (page 198)

$4 + 2 = 6$

$3 + 3 = 6$

What's the Problem? (page 199)

1. 3
2. 5
3. 5
4. 4
5. 4

Finish the Problems (page 200)

1. $3 - 1 = 2$
2. $5 - 2 = 3$
3. $3 - 3 = 0$

Big Problems with Bugs! (page 201)

1. $10 + 1 = 11$
2. $10 + 3 = 13$
3. $10 + 5 = 15$
4. $10 + 7 = 17$

Big Problems with Ants! (page 202)

1. $10 + 2 = 12$
2. $10 + 4 = 14$
3. $10 + 9 = 19$
4. $10 + 6 = 16$

Measure Up! (page 203)

1. 2 pencils
2. 6 pencils
3. 1 pencil

Measure and Compare (page 204)

Students' responses will vary.

Measure and Compare More (page 205)

1. 10 paper clips
2. 4 paper clips
3. 3 paper clips

Measure and Compare Big Things (page 206)

Students' responses will vary.

Sort and Count! (page 207)

1. 4 balls
2. 3 bats
3. 6 suns
4. 4 clouds

Sort and Count More! (page 208)

1. 5 pans
2. 5 eggs
3. 5 stars
4. 4 moons

Sort and Count by Size (page 209)

1. 3 little cars
2. 3 big cars
3. 5 big dogs
4. 3 little dogs

Sort and Count by Shape (page 210)

1. 3 circles
2. 3 squares
3. 3 food things
4. 4 play things

Find the Shapes (page 211)

1. b
2. b
3. b
4. b

Find More Shapes (page 212)

1. a
2. a
3. c
4. b

Where Are the Shapes? (page 213)

1. a
2. b
3. b
4. c

Answer Key *(cont.)*

Make the Shapes (page 214)

Students' responses will vary.

Name the Shapes (page 215)

Students should connect the names to the appropriate shapes.

Shape Match (page 216)

Students should connect the names to the appropriate shapes.

More Shape Naming (page 217)

Check activity sheets to see that students followed instructions.

Build with Shapes (page 218)

Check activity sheets to see that students followed instructions.

Flat or Solid? (page 219)

1. solid
2. flat
3. flat
4. solid
5. flat
6. solid

Flat and Solid Figures (page 220)

1. solid
2. flat
3. solid
4. flat
5. flat
6. flat

How Many Sides? (page 221)

1. sides of square are numbered 1–4; 4
2. sides of rectangle are numbered 1–4; 4
3. sides of triangle are numbered 1–3; 3

Count the Sides (page 222)

1. sides of rectangle are numbered 1–4; 4
2. sides of square are numbered 1–4; 4
3. sides of triangle are numbered 1–3; 3

Count More Sides (page 223)

1. sides of cube are numbered 1–6; 6
2. sides of rectangular prism are numbered 1–6; 6
3. sides of pyramid are numbered 1–5; 5

Count All the Sides (page 224)

1. 4
2. 6
3. 4
4. 6
5. 3
6. 5

Alike and Different Shapes (page 225)

1. They each have 4 sides.
2. The square has 4 equal sides and the rectangle has two sets of equal sides.

More Alike and Different Shapes (page 226)

1. They are both rectangular.
2. The rectangular prism has 6 sides and the rectangle has 4 sides.

Make Flat Shapes (page 227)

Students should trace all shapes.

Contents of the Resource CD

Contents of the Resource CD (cont.)

Contents of the Resource CD (cont.)

#50883—Bright & Brainy: Kindergarten Practice

Notes

Notes